Vintage Years

Books by William E. Hulme
Published by The Westminster Press

Vintage Years:
Growing Older with Meaning and Hope

Mid-Life Crises (Christian Care Books)

Vintage Years
Growing Older
with Meaning and Hope

William E. Hulme

The Westminster Press
Philadelphia

Scripture quotations from the Revised Standard Version of the Bible are copyrighted 1946, 1952, © 1971, 1973 by the Division of Christian Education of the National Council of the Churches of Christ in the U.S.A. and are used by permission.

Book design by Gene Harris

First edition

Published by The Westminster Press®
Philadelphia, Pennsylvania

PRINTED IN THE UNITED STATES OF AMERICA

9 8 7 6 5 4 3 2 1

Library of Congress Cataloging-in-Publication Data

Hulme, William Edward, 1920–
    Vintage years.

    1. Aged—Conduct of life. 2. Aged—Religious life.
I. Title.
BJ1691.H85 1986   248.4′841   85-26399
ISBN 0-664-24684-2 (pbk.)

Contents

CHAPTER 1
The Need for Meaning in Aging

When the seemingly invincible John McEnroe was decisively defeated and eliminated from the Wimbledon tennis tournament in 1985 by Kevin Curren, he said that at 26 he felt *old*. In his forty-fifth year, champion golfer Jack Nicklaus expressed frustration over his play: "The first day the greens were fast, today they were slow. You tell me what's going on? I don't understand." Sports columnist Patrick Reusse offered a suggestion. "Arnold Palmer can tell you what is going on, Jack. It's called getting older" ("Nicklaus Feeling His Age," *St. Paul Pioneer Press,* April 13, 1985, p. 7c).

What about you? Are you noting any signs of getting older? Do you lament at times that you can't do certain things the way you used to do them? Do you play out sooner? Do you have pains in your hands, shoulders, knees, hips, back? Do you despair and wonder where all the years have gone? Does the prospect of where the years are leading scare you? Do you envision being enfeebled in a nursing home, dependent on others, senile—perhaps like a grandparent, aunt, uncle, or even a parent?

It is understandable if this picture frightens you. It is a specter that challenges your sense of meaning. Your purpose for living, the values around which you have shaped your life, seem to collapse in such a future. Is this where it all ends? If so, what's the purpose of it all?

Perhaps you are already at that age called "old," which we prefer to call "vintage years." Where are *you* in your thinking? What is your "old age" doing to you?

What precisely are those years we call "old"? After 65? The president of the Blue Cross and Blue Shield Association, Bernard R. Tresnowski, has stated that there has been such a change in our recent population that our older years really begin at 75 rather than 65. This is probably not what you were led to believe at your place of work—or perhaps even by your physician.

Most of the time we joke about our aging symptoms. As our joints crack or we rise a little stiffly from the chair or forget something, we may pass it off if others are around by saying with a grin, "I must be getting old." Underneath, we may not be grinning. We may be envisioning the ominous wheelchair, crippled arthritic joints, a nursing home with people all around us who are senile and decrepit.

What Happens as We Age

Is this picture of aging in our culture a realistic one? Most of us would probably say yes. Are there no advantages in this movement of the years? Again, most of us would probably say no. "Hopeless, passive, uninvolved, fragile." This is how young adults view older people, according to Ralph Kahana's study of 124 subjects across the age spectrum. Ironically, the elderly view themselves in similar negative terms and also add the adjective lonely. (One has to be elderly to know about the loneliness.) On the other hand, young adulthood is viewed by all groups as the most desirable age. Even older people see young adults as "hardy, active, independent, and involved." As one might anticipate, the older years are viewed by all age groups as the least desirable. "It is clear," says Kahana, "that the elderly share society's worship of youth" (quoted in John R. Barry and C. Ray Wingrove, eds., *Let's Learn About Aging*, p. 129; Schenkman Publishing Co., 1977). Aging viewed from this perspective obviously threatens our need to live meaningfully.

The purpose of this book is to present another perspective—one that challenges this dim view of the aging process. But first we need to look at how aging affects us in our society.

Aging, in our culture, is seen as reversing the course of growth. Things cease to be "ever-expanding" as we age and become "ever-decreasing." For Americans, meaning stems from growth. Our emphasis on the gross national product, by which we measure our economic and thus our national health, has led to a GNP cultural mentality. We fail to reckon with life that is going the other way. This tendency is reflected in our denial of death, which Ernest Becker saw as the pervading characteristic of our culture (*The Denial of Death*, Free Press, 1973). The situation has become better in this regard since Becker published his analysis (perhaps to some extent because of it). Yet as long as our culture itself continues to identify meaning with growth and expansion, there is a built-in impediment to finding meaning in death and aging.

A scientific analysis of aging reveals that aging is indeed a slowing-down process. The physiological activities of the body inevitably decline. During physical exercise, the amount of blood pumped by the heart per minute is less in the older person than in the younger one and the amount of oxygen that the blood takes up from the lungs and carries to the tissues also declines. Of course, there is less blood per minute flowing through the lungs of the elderly, but the lung tissue itself has changed. Similarly, the amount of blood passing through the kidneys decreases. Yet in this as in other differences, some 80-year-olds may show no more decline than the average 50-year-old. We will investigate these differences among people in later chapters. The overall slow-down in body functions, however, means that older people need more time to return to normal after exercise than younger persons.

Other changes also take place. There is a decreased elevation of adrenal activity in older persons, meaning that the elderly have a reduced capacity for coping with stress. The number of nerve trunk fibers decreases by 37 percent in the bodies of the elderly, accounting to some degree for the decline in the complex connections of the central nervous system. Our senses also may decline with age. The sense of taste sustains the most extensive loss. The number of taste buds per papilla of the tongue can go from an average of 245 in young people to only 88 in people of advanced years.

The weight of our body organs also decreases. The brain, for example, in older persons may weigh as much as 44 percent less than the brain of younger people. This weight loss is due to the loss of tissue caused by the death and disappearance of body cells. In fact, the aging process is often described as a reduction in the number of cells in the body. This also means a loss of muscle fibers, with a resulting decrease in physical strength.

As we age, the reserve capacities in our body—our ability to return to normal after disturbances in our equilibrium caused by strains and stresses—is reduced. The fact that Ronald Reagan in his seventies could bounce back so quickly after surgery shows how "un-aged" was his body. Ultimately, however, this reduction does occur, and as disease, incapacity, and just the stress of daily living impose more demands on our shrinking reserve capacities, our body begins to die.

Even if we believe that a decline in cells is responsible for aging, what causes the number of our cells to decline? Are there changes taking place in the internal metabolism of the cell that damage its capacity for repair and for reproduction? Does aging affect the enzyme activity within cells, which in turn leads to these other changes? It is in these and other areas that the scientific research into aging is currently directed.

Aging as Indigenous to Nature

Although we think of the elderly when we refer to aging, the aging process actually begins much earlier. We see this clearly in the life span of a professional athlete. Baseball pitchers, as they age, learn to "pitch with their heads" to make up for a loss in physical power. Older athletes are frequently called "ageless wonders" by the media. Lou Groza in football, Billie Jean King in tennis, Bobby Hull in hockey, Warren Spahn, Satchel Paige, Gaylord Perry in baseball: these players are examples of those who stretched the age limits in their careers. But ageless wonders they were not and are not. They all reached the time when they could no longer compete with younger athletes. Decline in athletic prowess is as sure as death, for the simple reason that it is a stage in the same process.

If there were no aging, there would also probably be no death. And without death could there be birth? If there is no ending, can there be a beginning? Can you imagine what it would be like if mosquitoes only hatched but never died? Could we humans survive? Could we survive if humans were born but never died? We can postpone death more and more to the later years, but the death rate is still 100 percent. Ultimately the system—life—breaks down and dies.

Even though we are part of nature and nature needs death for life, in our *human* nature we protest death. Rather than being needed for life, death seems to be a threat to life, and consequently a threat to growth and meaning.

In our day of the postponement of death to the later years, youth, with the exception of those involved in war, can look to the future in our industrialized countries as an almost endless time in which to hope and to dream. Of course, death is acknowledged as one's final destiny, but with abundant years in between, this acknowledgment can remain abstract. In contrast, as one moves along through life, the time remaining to us obviously becomes less abundant. In fact, its speed of passage seems to increase. Obviously it doesn't—since there are still twenty-four hours in a day—but subjectively time "flies." The 24-hour day becomes a smaller and smaller percentage of one's life. When I think of my college years, they seem to have been a major epoch in my life. Yet there were only four of these years. Now, when I think of the past four years as a comparison, they seem to be a much shorter period.

This different perspective of time between one generation and another comes to the fore for our family at our family reunions. These are held in various parts of the country, depending upon where the host relative happens to live. My wife and I prefer to fly to these places rather than spend three to four days driving. But we cannot persuade my son and his wife to accompany us. Because of the greater expense of flying for the two of them, they prefer to drive. For us, in our particular age and life situation, time is more valuable than money. For the younger generation, struggling financially to stay afloat and with a larger time span ahead in which to get things done, money is more valuable than time.

Losses: Little Deaths

The losses experienced as we age are reminders of the great loss to come: of our life. Reflecting on these losses, elder theologian Joseph Sittler says, "We are instructed in the fact and inevitability of our own death by the little deaths in our personal world" (quoted in Arthur H. Becker, "Pastoral/Theological Implications of the Aging Process," *SPC Journal,* vol. 7, 1985, p. 28). Many of these "little deaths" are the decline and sometimes cessation of the physiological processes of our bodies described previously. Sittler, for example, is nearly blind.

Some physicians use the word "degenerative" in describing the changes in the body due to aging. This word can become prescriptive as well; it conjures up scary mental pictures of our bodies that are anything but healing. "Degenerative" can be a devastating word. It is opposite in meaning to "regenerative." The contrast is obviously between life and death, creation and destruction. This is one example of the role the practice of medicine has at times played in the negative programming for aging, a subject we will discuss further in chapter 4.

The losses of aging are also the reverse of the acquisition that characterizes our cultural understanding of meaning as growth—in this case the growth of our gross *personal* product, which in turn leads to increased acquisitions. These acquisitions are signs of our success, but in the retirement years one may experience the *decline* of these resources. Speaking from experience on this subject for his church forum, a retiree said, "We experience losses throughout life. From the time of retirement the number of losses we experience increases with ever greater frequency. Before retirement our lives were a period of acquisition in the form of greater economic resources, position, influence, authority, and friends. At retirement we lose position and all that entails. Sooner or later we lose significant others through ill health or death. We may lose our own health and strength, and the independence that goes with them. Roles once enjoyed quietly slip away."

How many retirees have discovered to their chagrin that the comfortable nest egg that was supposed to carry them through their senior years has been eroded by a series of illnesses? The irony is that only after their own resources (acquisitions) have been exhausted can they receive basic aid from government.

Losses, or little deaths, apply also to our intellectual abilities. One of the great fears of aging is senility. One of the most baffling diseases—Alzheimer's and related degenerative brain diseases—is now thought to cause some of the mental deterioration of the elderly. Yet some is caused also by the aging process in the brain, which accelerates, it seems, when traumas like illness, hospitalization, and loss of loved ones disturb the needed familiarity of place, persons, and routine.

An elderly woman who fell in her home and severely injured herself found it difficult to remember words and names when the hospital chaplain called on her. "I can't seem to remember what I obviously should know," she said. What she did know, however, and what may have further traumatized her, was that her first duty after she left the hospital was to join her daughter in sorting through her things because it had been decided she could no longer live alone. "I don't want to do that—I just don't! Yet what else can I do?" She sighed. "Sometimes I think I am coming apart at the seams."

Older people often believe that society is also coming apart at the seams. The familiar lament of the aged is that people and customs are not what they used to be. People are not as trustworthy and customs are no longer structures for caring. The society that once included them in is now leaving them out. Where once they received affirmation, now they receive rejection.

"Coming apart at the seams" is remarkably similar to a lament frequently expressed by those in the throes of a mid-life crisis: "I feel like I'm going to pieces." Both expressions are graphic descriptions of a process that is both traumatic and destructive. They convey the opposite of building up, growing, expanding—words that denote meaning, purpose, and even life itself.

Included in this fear of aging, erroneously, is the fear of *sexual* death, particularly for men. So closely is sex associated with life that Freud called it the life instinct as opposed to the death instinct. Its demise in later years would be a triumph of death over life, of meaningless over meaning, of emptiness over fulfillment. This, of course, is particularly true in a culture which puts sex along with youth as the epitome of human aspiration.

The meaninglessness associated with aging contributes to a spiritual crisis. The infliction of losses leads those who grieve over them to question the wisdom, the love, the care, and even the very existence of God. Arthur Becker says it well: "What is particularly agonizing about suffering is the fear that it somehow may be evidence that one is no longer in God's care. . . . What sufferers long for is assurance that God has not abandoned them" (loc. cit., p. 29). For many people, providence—God's care— is synonymous with meaning. When one's faith is shaken—when one wonders instead whether one has been abandoned by God, by the universe—the anxiety of meaninglessness reaches the stage of despair.

Aging as Progression Toward Death

Aging in our culture is seen as the process that puts an end to life—a slow progression toward death. My own experience of this perception came early. My aged grandfather lived with us when I was a child. He was weary of living, and at bedtime, as I said good night to him, he would ask me to pray that he would not be there in the morning. My grandmother was less dramatic. As the day ended, she would just say, "We are one day closer to our grave." This daily reminder of death as a threat to life—*my* life—and life's meaning—*my* life's meaning— feeds into our basic fear of death. Ironically, what is meaningful in nature—in fact, nature depends on it—is meaningless, even destructive, to human nature.

As we have noted, our mental pictures of the aged are frequently those of "the frail old," even though most of the elderly are not in this category. This negative focus is similar to the notion that most old people live in homes for the aged, though this is the case for only about 7 percent. Some of the elderly, however, *are* the frail old. The pastor of one of my former colleagues informed me of the deteriorated condition of this scholarly man, now in his nineties. "He is now only a shell of the person you once knew," he said. I was saddened to hear this, and my immediate wish was that my old colleague could die. I related this experience to a friend, and she gently reminded me that I was not reckoning with the total picture. "How do you know," she said, "that he is not living even now for a purpose?" Even the frail old are not necessarily living meaningless lives. When I reflected on this, I realized that what saddened me—in addition to my colleague's state—was that such a condition is a possibility for all who live to old age. I too am confronted with this destiny. Obviously this is a threat to my need for control over my life. When control is lost, is not meaning also? Hence death, despite its ending to life, is preferred to a *meaningless* life.

The Big Fear—Loss of Control

We fear the loss of control in aging—a foreshadowing of the complete loss of control in dying. Whenever we fear the loss of control, we are tempted to *take* control in negative ways. Acts of violence, for example, are often irrational reactions to a loss of control. If we cannot control something or someone constructively, we may in desperation seek to control them destructively. Herein is the distorted appeal of suicide. Although one is in fear of death, one has little control over when and how it will come, unless one seizes destructive control and takes one's own life. The suicide pacts that people make regarding the ominous future are frequently of this nature. The example of the former president of Union Theological Seminary, Henry Van Dusen and his wife, are frequently cited. They agreed to die together by their own hand when the aging process threatened the meaning, the control, of their lives. When they perceived that this time had come, they committed suicide together.

Right of Way by Richard Lees is a play on this same theme. In the play, however, the aged couple—the wife is terminally ill—is stopped in their suicide attempt by a well-meaning daughter and societal authorities. What they offer the aged couple, instead, is a meaningless existence of living in institutions, separated from each other. Besides being a dramatization of the frustrations of aging, the play is also a social criticism of the way our society treats its elderly. The play is so skillful in its presentation that as I watched the performance I found myself to my amazement actually hoping that the elderly couple would be able to pull it off.

The loss of control in the frail old is symbolized in the embarrassing, even humiliating, loss of continence. A prominent movie actor known for tough-guy roles, in which he was always in control, lived long enough to lament what he described as "this degrading experience of getting old."

In addition to incontinence, the prospect of dying slowly in old age is another threat to one's control. Dr. Benjamin Spock in his eighty-first year wrote an article for *Parade* magazine entitled "A Way to Say Farewell." In it he described how he would like to die. "When I wonder what directions to leave, I realize that, in addition to my own wishes, there will be my wife's feelings and my doctor's ethics to consider. For instance, even though I've decided in advance that I want to be put out of my misery if the pain proves unbearable, will my doctor be willing to give the necessary dose of medication—or to leave it handy—and will Mary [his wife] have the nerve to jab the needle?" (*Parade*, March 10, 1985, p. 10). In using these words he was saying that he wanted to be treated like a pet animal. I was reminded as I read this of the title of a motion picture depicting life in the Great Depression entitled, *They Shoot Horses, Don't They?* In the film these words were spoken by a young man frustrated by poverty and hopelessness to justify the voluntary taking of human life when life ceases to hold meaning.

The Growth Dimension to Aging

There is growth in aging, but our culture is unable to recognize it. In his second letter to the Corinthians, Paul described this growth in the midst of apparent decline. "So we do not lose heart. Though our outer nature is wasting away, our inner nature is being renewed every day" (2 Cor. 4:16). Though our body tissues decline through the loss of cells, our spirit is developing in the opposite direction. It is not stymied by the decline of the body, but rather is renewed in the daily drain on the body's energy, so that one can cope positively with the aging process. "For this slight momentary affliction is preparing for us an eternal weight of glory beyond all comparison" (2 Cor. 4:17). Although in one sense our destination is the grave, in another it is eternal glory. Our spirits are renewed as we see in the earthly affliction that leads to the grave the guiding hand of God to the eternal fulfillment of life.

While spiritual renewal helps us cope with the other- wise meaningless decline in our minds and bodies, spiritual renewal is in itself a healing influence for both mind and body. Even as the body and mind are affected negatively in their functioning by despair, so also they are affected positively in their functioning by hope. The eternal dimension in the spirit's vision provides this hope.

Obviously, in the second half of life we need a

perspective that includes death so that we can come to terms with it. Those who have had a close brush with death, who have faced it concretely rather than abstractly, often come to peace with it in ways that would be difficult without this experience. A close friend of mine had the experience in his young adulthood. "Since then," he said, "every day is grace." A student of mine, though a young man, lived for several weeks with a diagnosis of illness that held no hope for recovery. Although this diagnosis was later proved to be wrong and he recovered fully, he looks upon this short period of his life as his most shaping influence. "I learned," he said, "what it means to live *today*."

Community life, family tradition, and religion all provide us solace when facing death. For many people, these sources for support no longer have the place in society that they once had. Without these resources we are left on our own precisely when we feel most empty. Hence, the ready connection between emptiness and meaninglessness, which we shall discuss further in the next chapter.

In the face of this threat to meaning implied in our dying, researcher Kahana says that our challenge as we age is "to maintain a positive self-image in the face of a thankless and devalued position" (*Let's Learn About Aging*, p. 131). This is certainly one way of describing what it means to grow older meaningfully, and this is precisely the challenge concerning which we shall attempt to be helpful in this book. But we also need to work at the other end—the cultural-social end. Old age ought *not* to be a thankless and devalued position, and we shall attempt to be helpful here also in the challenge to change this situation in our society. But first we need to examine the particular role of meaning and of its opposite, meaninglessness, in our contemporary society, within which our own personal experience with these conditions is primarily a reflection.

CHAPTER 2
The Anxiety of Meaninglessness

Despair is the ultimate response to meaninglessness. This is because meaninglessness and hopelessness go together. Sadness, sorrow, and depression turn into despair when we lose hope. Although we may feel far removed from Jesus when we despair, the fact is that Jesus himself experienced despair. "My God, my God, why hast thou forsaken me?" This cry of Jesus from the cross expressed the agony of the disillusioned. All his disciples had left him at his arrest. Now, at his execution, the last straw of meaning was breaking. God, it seemed, had joined the forsakers. Jesus felt abandoned—let down—betrayed.

It was a human cry. Perhaps you have cried it yourself, or at least felt like it. Perhaps you are feeling this way now. A woman I know felt this way when she broke her hip at age 85 and faced the ominous end of independent living. A middle-aged farmer felt this way when his wife left him after twenty-five years of marriage. Another felt this way over the closing of the factory for which he had worked as a foreman for many years, leaving him unemployed at 55. This feeling is despair.

In crying these words Jesus was identifying with another sufferer, the author of Psalm 22, who expressed the same lament: "My God, my God, why hast thou forsaken me? Why art thou so far from helping me, from the words of my groaning?" (Ps. 22:1). You can find almost any feeling you are experiencing expressed in the psalms. Here it is the feeling of abandonment. Jesus also could have used the words of Job, who symbolizes all sufferers as they search desperately for direction, for meaning. "Thy hands fashioned and made me," Job cried out to God, "and now thou dost turn about and destroy me" (Job 10:8).

Psychoanalyst Carl Jung in *Answer to Job* says that Job's charge against God was justified and God knew it. Even though Job finally made his peace with God, God realized that Job's charge against him was not really answered. So to ease his conscience God decided to become incarnate—to join the human race—which he did in the person of Jesus. So in Jesus' sufferings as they climax on the cross, God was actually taking Job's place (*Answer to Job*; London: Routlege & Kegan Paul, 1954).

As tongue-in-cheek as this description of God's actions sounds, it is remarkably similar to the New Testament description of God's compassion for our sufferings: namely, that God *identified* with them. If Jesus is the person through whom God identified with humanity, he needed to endure what we humans endure—he could not be spared the most painful of such endurances. In the words of the Letter to the Hebrews, "He had to be made like his brethren in every respect" (2:17). If he was "to sympathize with our weaknesses," he must be "one who in every respect has been tempted as we are" (4:15). Therefore he had to endure the most severe of all temptations or trials, the despair of forsakenness—of abandonment.

Collapse of Direction

When that which we had counted on to give meaning to our lives collapses into the chaos of meaninglessness, our response, as we have noted, is despair. Danish theologian Søren Kierkegaard said it is our advantage over the beasts that we *can* despair. This distinguishes us as a species, he says, far more than the erect posture in which we carry our bodies, "for it implies the infinite erectness or loftiness of being spirit" (*The Sickness Unto Death,* p. 148; Princeton University Press, reprinted 1980). Identifying despair with hopelessness, novelist Graham Greene puts it similarly: "Hope is an instinct only the reasoning mind can kill. An animal never knows despair" (*The Power and the Glory,* p. 141; Penguin Books, 1962).

Despair is the agony of all agonies. Theologian Paul Tillich says it is the "boundary-line situation. One cannot go beyond it" (*Courage to Be,* p. 54; Yale University Press, 1953). If you have been there, you know where this boundary is. It's as though all sense of direction had vanished. As in the familiar analogy of being lost in the woods, you thought you were going in the right direction, that you were headed out of the woods; then the moment of truth arrives when you see the telltale signs—you've been this way before, you are back where you began. You're going in circles—going nowhere—lost in the woods.

Perhaps you, like Jesus, were trusting providence, and now providence seems to have gone into reverse. "My God, where are you? Who are you? Is there any use? What's the sense of it all when nothing makes sense?" This is despair, the anxiety of meaninglessness. Kierkegaard called it a sickness in the spirit, in the self—a "sickness unto death." He used the fable of the knight who pursued the rare bird as an analogy of despair. The knight pursued the bird because it was so close. But just as he would be about to seize it, the bird would fly just beyond his reach. He pursued this tantalizing quest until darkness overtook him and he became ominously aware that he no longer knew where he was (*Sickness Unto Death,* p. 170).

Once we've known the lostness, the sinking feeling, the

dread of despair, we never want to know it again. "All human life," says Tillich, "can be interpreted as a continuous attempt to avoid despair" (*Courage to Be*, p. 56). Yet despair periodically threatens to close in on us, to crowd us into a corner where we cannot get out. Or it may seem to do the opposite: threaten to thrust us into a vast no-man's-land where we cannot find our way.

Both threats are experienced in the familiar imagery of nightmares. Have you ever dreamed that you couldn't get your sluggish legs moving fast enough to prevent being overtaken by a pursuing danger? This is the dread of being closed in. In the open-ended dream you feel you are slipping off, falling into endless space.

It was in the *wakened* nightmare of the Nazi concentration camps that psychiatrist Viktor Frankl perceived the insight that established the basis for his logotherapy. Can you imagine any time or place in which it would be more impossible to preserve a sense of meaning than as a Jew in the Holocaust? Yet it was in the concentration camp that Frankl experienced and witnessed the indispensable role of meaning for survival. When we lose this meaning, we become overwhelmed with futility. We cannot live this way for long. It is not humanly possible. We need meaning to survive.

In their common experience of abandonment, Job, the psalmist, and Jesus all endured the spiritual onslaught of meaninglessness. Because of the severity of their pain—mental, physical, spiritual—they could not distract themselves from the temptation to despair. The questions that tormented them were indeed dreadful. Were they abandoned by the human community, by the universe, by God? As they fought to retain hope, despair kept pressing in upon them.

Periods of Anxiety

Tillich believes that this anxiety of meaninglessness, to which he also adds emptiness, is the dominant anxiety of our age. There were periods of great anxiety before, but they were different in emphasis. Historically, each period of anxiety followed the end of an epoch. It is in periods of transition, when former traditions are no longer relied on, that people's anxieties are heightened. Tillich identifies three such periods during the Christian era of Western civilization: the end of the Republic in the Roman empire, the end of the Middle Ages in Europe, and the end of the modern era in our time.

In the first period the dominant anxiety was primarily over fate and death. Death is both the symbol and the epitome of all endings, and therefore a threat to all meaning in *life*. Aging, with its symptoms of approaching death, illness and infirmity, is a fateful reminder of our destiny in death. Both death and aging are inevitable, the denouncement of fate, beyond human control.

The Stoic philosophers responded to this anxiety by exerting the only control left to human beings. While they could not prevent either their aging or their dying, they could control their attitude toward both. Their approach was to control one's *passions* or emotions—specifically, one's anxiety—by accepting without complaint whatever fate or the divine will ordained. Frankl developed a similar approach to the Nazi concentration camp. Obviously, the inmates of these death camps could exert no control over anything that might happen to them, but they could exert control over their own attitude toward their miserable lot. The exercise of this control is the last freedom that humans possess, and no one, not even Nazi sadists, could take it from them. The Christian response to this anxiety of fate and death was the good news of the resurrection of Christ.

The predominant anxiety of the second period is the

anxiety of guilt and condemnation. The centuries of the Christian era had brought to its adherents an acute sense of moral accountability. By the end of the Middle Ages the traditional ways of the church for dealing with the guilt of the people over their failures in this accountability were losing their effectiveness. The Renaissance popes who governed the church during this transitional period were so thoroughly corrupt and secular that people lost respect for them and for many of the priests who served under them. So when the traditional ways of this priesthood for allaying the guilt of the people were no longer effective, many of the people felt rejected by God because of their unresolved guilt—they felt condemned. A psalm again describes this anxiety: "The pains of Sheol laid hold on me" (Ps. 116:3, KJV). The Reformation with its proclamation of the grace and forgiveness of God was a response to this prevalent anxiety of guilt and condemnation.

The Anxiety of Our Era

In contrast to the period of the Reformation, our own day is not characterized by any acute moral conscience but rather more by its opposite—a disintegration of moral consciousness. This, says Tillich, leads to meaninglessness. Our anxiety is aroused by this loss of a spiritual center. There are no answers to the perpetual questions we humans raise about the meaning of our existence. But this does not imply that we have given up the search. Rather, it only increases our desperation in that search. We go from one promised panacea to another, as the hoped-for meaning in each tends ultimately to vanish in the heat of reality. As Tillich puts it, "Everything is tried and nothing satisfies" (*Courage to Be*, p. 48). The anxiety of meaninglessness lurks at the horizon of our consciousness. So we latch on to whatever current fad promises to ease it.

This is illustrated by the short-lived popularity of the many guru-oriented philosophies associated with what is loosely called the human potential movement. This is a movement for self-fulfillment, or what psychologist Abraham Maslow called self-actualization. I spent a sabbatical year in researching—through personal involvement—several forms of this movement, which are usually a particular mix of psychotherapy and spirituality. They are short-lived not because they have no value—I found the majority of them valuable for me—but because either their leaders or their adherents have claimed too much for them. They can enhance our sense of meaning—they certainly did for me—but they cannot provide us with this meaning. I brought Christian meaning with me and profited. But if I had come to those workshops and seminars to find meaning, I believe I would ultimately have been disillusioned. The emptiness then experienced is exacerbated by fallen hopes.

While the offerings of the human potential movement are a contemporary example of the search for meaning, the appeal of older options is still strong. One option, as old as recorded history, is to throw oneself into whatever pleasures are available at the moment with no thought of future consequences. This is because thoughts of the future raise questions about meaning, whereas the pleasure of the moment provides sufficient meaning for *now*. While we usually think of sexual pleasures in this regard, it is only one of many others, such as the pleasure one may receive from shopping sprees, bargain-hunting, indulging in tasty foods, or exerting power over another person or persons. Because pleasure in itself is good, this way has a strong appeal—if one does not deal with matters of motivation and subsequent consequences.

In describing the attraction of TV star Joan Collins, *Parade* magazine notes that the public "imagines her to be the freewheeling hedonist that most people are afraid to be." The fact that at this writing Joan is 51 years old and a TV sex symbol with a real-life lover fourteen years her junior may also provide the illusion that she has successfully defied the threat of aging. Collins does not disperse this illusion by her own comments on aging. "I tell you, age is no big thing unless you make it so. It's more a state of mind." Obviously behind the anxiety of meaninglessness and emptiness is the anxiety of fate and death (Joan Collins, "On Choosing a Younger Man," *Parade*, Dec. 23, 1984, p. 14).

Work offers another age-old route for the search for meaning. In our day we refer to those who pursue this route as workaholics. This addiction affects primarily men in our culture, since work has been the way offered to men to establish their worth, although this situation is now changing to include women. You may know this route by experience. Or at least you may know of the up-and-coming man who devotes his time and energies and mental preoccupation largely to his work, leaving family obligations mostly to his spouse, and leaving unsatisfied his own needs for leisure and intimacy. The illusion is that the business, the status, the salary, the importance of the work to society provide one's own life with sufficient meaning.

The aging process works against this as well as against other questionable ways of finding meaning. In the latter half of life we ask questions about meaning and destiny that the work route alone cannot answer. Even people in religious professions can fall victim to this illusion about their work—even theological professors! Pastoral theologian Wayne Oates, for example, has a book entitled *Confessions of a Workaholic* (World Publishing Co., 1971). The late neo-orthodox theologian Reinhold Niebuhr is another example. He was sidelined by a stroke in his later years and received an insight during this time into his mixture of motives regarding his demanding speaking schedule. "Retrospection from the sidelines," he wrote, "prompted me to remember many instances in my

earlier years when my wife protested my making an extra
trip or going to yet another conference, despite my
weariness: I always pleaded the importance of the cause
that engaged me, and it never occurred to me that I
might have been so assiduous in these engagements
because the invitation flattered my vanity" ("View of Life
from the Sidelines," *The Christian Century*, Dec. 19–26,
1984, pp. 1196–1197).

Having a value system based on competitive striving to
establish personal worth, our society fosters this illusion
that the way to allay the anxiety of meaninglessness and
emptiness is through hard work. The grass on the other
side of the fence spurs on the competition because it is
always greener. As long as someone has more than I, I
will keep on striving. This competitive pressure possesses
labor as well as management. A well-known labor leader,
when asked what labor really wants, said, "More!" Meaning is *more*. The illusion is apparent. If meaning is more,
then satisfaction, fulfillment, is really impossible. The
threat of emptiness is always included within the anxiety
of meaninglessness.

Another age-old option in the search for meaning that
still has its appeal in spite of our so-called hardheaded
realism is romanticism. Romanticism is implicit in an
economic system in which acquisition is the route to
personal fulfillment. One's ambition, therefore, is to
acquire, to achieve, to possess. To be able to purchase the
proper automobile or automobiles, the fitting house or
houses, or to successfully woo and win the idealized
person is the pursuit that promises fulfillment. The
illusion is exposed after we acquire either the desired
possession or person, for the anticipated fulfillment is
short lived. In spite of this the quest goes on.

Not only the young are susceptible to romantic illu-
sions. The middle-aged also may latch on to this option.
Perhaps the growing anxiety over the aging process
during mid-life is behind this susceptibility to romanti-

cism. By now, the acquisition of *things* may have lost some of its appeal to the acquisition of a *person*. As one enters into the second half of life, with its destination of death, the hope for escape may lie in a *new* relationship reminiscent of youthful romanticism.

Ann is an example of such a quest. Married to the same man for twenty-seven years, successful in her job as an office manager, blessed with children who have caused her few problems, Ann became bored with her life. Boredom is often the way the anxiety of meaninglessness and emptiness manifests itself. Ann was an "incurable romantic" and, despite her convictions regarding marital fidelity, was at this time of her life subconsciously open to an affair. Although she was anything but a promiscuous person, she ambivalently longed for a new love relationship as the answer to her boredom. Since she was open to the possibility, the possibility developed. Only a forgiving and caring spouse and concerned and loving children prevented her from taking the decisive step of divorce and remarriage in two subsequent affairs. Torn in this way in two directions, Ann on her down days felt doomed to a frustrating stalemate.

Dave pursued careers like Ann desired a lover. He changed his career plans five times in ten years. Each new option promised the hoped-for panacea until reality set in. After a while the flaws in the new situation become apparent, and old frustrations simply took on a new setting. Instead of dispersing the illusion, however, the discontent simply shifted his attention to another career possibility. But as Dave ages, opportunities for these new possibilities will become fewer and fewer. Then what does one do with one's job frustration? One's personal dissatisfaction with one's life? Thus the anxiety of emptiness drives one to the abyss of meaninglessness, where the romantic illusion dies, but dies hard, as time begins to run out.

We cannot at this time see where or if the Christian

gospel will meet the needs behind the current anxiety of meaninglessness and emptiness as it has with the anxieties of previous periods in Western civilization. We cannot yet see that history in retrospect. This book is a description of what the gospel *could* say or mean to our period of transition. But the jury is still out on whether it will do so.

Changes Since Tillich's Analysis

There have been many changes in our society since Tillich made his analysis of our dominant anxiety. Yet this anxiety has continued through them all. Tillich's view is showing itself throughout these changes to be relevant and valid.

The area that most clearly reveals these changes is the youth subculture. During the fifties, after the Korean War, young people were described as seeking personal security above everything else. They were content to settle for a niche on the side of the mountain. During the sixties the counterculture movement, abetted by the Vietnam War, was a rebellion of youth, particularly middle-class youth, against the materialistic and success-oriented goals of their elders. As the seventies passed into the eighties, the counterculture movement was absorbed into the culture at large, and a new group of young people has emerged who in considerable numbers have espoused the old economic goals of acquisition and desire again to climb to the top of the mountain of prosperity as they emulate their older models, the young urban professionals. But there are echoes of the sixties in current student protests against apartheid in South Africa and U.S. intervention in Central America.

The older economic goal of acquisition is in a new setting. Ours is an age of increased choices, which stimulates the anxiety implicit in freedom. The young are more free today from cultural structures and pressures to decide whether or not to get married, to have babies. They are more free to choose alternative lifestyles, now that the social pressures against such choices have considerably lessened. The authority for these new decisions regarding how one shall shape one's life is in *oneself.* So also the consequences of these decisions likewise must be borne by oneself. This, of course, can be frightening since we are not that confident of any ground of authority in ourselves.

Ironically, the options that promise us more control of our lives arouse within us the fear of losing control. In any transitional period which lacks the moral and ethical standards that give support for specific options, we are afraid our decisions may lead us into chaos rather than meaning. Our control over our lives then seems to be illusory. Since a show of force, regardless of how irrational, looks like an assertion of control, we are prone to acts of violence against property and against persons. The violence of family abuse over which we are rightly concerned stems in part from a sense of powerlessness.

This need to exert control is evident even at the national level. The Vietnam War left us confused as a nation. There was no solution, no victory parade for the soldiers. There was only a prolonged and seemingly inevitable defeat. We have chafed under this powerlessness in subsequent events of national frustration—the Iranian hostage crisis, for example. We needed some evidence that we still controlled our national destiny. Regardless of how one interprets the invasion of Grenada, it was obviously a relatively safe show of force. We badly needed to *win* one. It restored some of our self-confidence as a powerful nation.

The Change to Secularism

A contributing factor to our anxiety of meaninglessness is that religion as it has been traditionally understood in our society is no longer built into our cultural values. Within just a few years, for example, a public school that annually had held its own Christmas program, complete with the nativity story and Christmas carols, could no longer even permit its teachers to wish their pupils Merry Christmas. When my high school son wrote a protest against this restriction for his school newspaper, he was called into the principal's office for a reprimand. There has been, however, no vacuum left by the loss. Secularism, with its apparent absence of any vertical or transcendent dimension to human living, has taken its place.

Two media presentations depicting nuclear war, *The Day After* and *Testament,* are striking examples of the effects of this secularization of our society. In the midst of the impending holocaust, none of the central characters in either drama are shown resorting to prayer or to worship for support. None of the conversations between those awaiting death ever refer to religious faith. Of course these are dramas, and the secularization is in the approach of the writers. Yet the fact that this approach could be presented as reflecting our culture is significant.

The very nature of holocausts seems to deny the reality of a transcendent world. It was because of the Holocaust of the Jews in Europe during the Nazi era that Rabbi Richard Rubenstein reached his conclusion that God is dead (Rubenstein, *After Auschwitz*; Bobbs-Merrill Co., 1966). In like manner the destruction of life on this planet through nuclear war evidently seems to include both God and eternity in its destruction.

Yet it was an actual surviver of the Holocaust, Viktor Frankl, to whom we previously referred, who, upon his release from the concentration camp at the end of World War II, fell to his knees in a religious expression of gratitude. "I stopped, looked around, and up to the sky—and then I went down on my knees. At that moment there was very little I knew of myself or of the world—

I had but one sentence in mind—always the same: I called to the Lord from my narrow prison and He answered me in the freedom of space. How long I knelt there and repeated this sentence memory can no longer recall. But I know that on that day, in that hour, my new life started" (*Man's Search for Meaning*, p. 142; Washington Square Press, 1963).

Attitudes Toward Leadership

Another way to note the changes since Tillich gave his analysis is in our attitude toward leadership. Although we have always idealized the rebel more than the authority, our respect for national leadership in recent decades has gone down and up like a roller coaster. What our Presidents, for example, have accomplished has seemed less important than the confidence they were able to inspire. The short presidency of John F. Kennedy is an example. However, in a few years we went from this high point of respect for the presidency to the credibility gap that began with the Johnson Administration and carried through into Ronald Reagan's presidency.

The major factor in this slide was the Vietnam War. The impression given to us as a society through the grisly evidence of body count was that we were winning the war. Yet this turned out to be an illusion. The reason given for escalating the war in the first place—an incident in the Tonkin Gulf—turned out later to be largely a deception. The ultimate defeat, as we have noted, took its toll on our national respect.

Then came Watergate and the ignominious end to the Nixon presidency. The short presidencies of Ford and Carter were unable to halt the slide. The hot topic in academe in those years was the "twilight of the presidency." This is no longer relevant. The turnabout came with the Reagan presidency. William Schneider, a resident at the American Enterprise Institute, notes that the election of Reagan was motivated by a national need for *change* but that his reelection was motivated by the need for *continuity* (Larry Eichel, "Has Reagan Really Changed America?" St. Paul *Dispatch,* Jan. 20, 1985, p. 1A)

What accounted for this rise in presidential prestige? Historian James McGregor Burns says it was a "phenomenon rarely seen in American politics": namely, "an idealogue with charm" (ibid.). As the person of Kennedy was more important than what he accomplished, which legislatively was very little, so the person of Reagan was more important than his political views. This was shown over and over by polls during his reelection campaign, which revealed that a majority of people disagreed with Reagan on many of his policies, yet they were determined to vote for him nevertheless. He had restored national confidence, and this was what the electorate wanted to see continued. One might say that Reagan resuscitated the myth of America's being the land of opportunity for the self-reliant.

Anxiety of Meaninglessness Remains

Yet in spite of this rise of optimism for the previous pessimism, of patriotism for the prior malaise, the anxiety of meaninglessness remains at the rim of consciousness. Christian faith, says C. S. Lewis, "does not begin with joy, but rather in despair. And it is no good trying to reach the joy without first going through the despair" (quoted in William H. Willimon, "Going Against the Stream," *Christian Century,* Dec. 19–26, 1984, p. 1193). Rather than going through the despair, have we not pulled back from it? Repentance for national sins, as well as for personal sins, is out of vogue. We have told ourselves that we are OK and that is it! Yet the latent fear of our internal chaos is still present. Our drug and alcohol dependency continues at its devastating pace. For many, life without chemicals is evidently empty.

Nor does it help to look back. We were never as good as we look in retrospect. Because institutions of the past were supported by popularly held values, however, they *did* provide a certain stability. Things certainly seemed better. People in the entertainment world, for example, did not say in public that they were living together without marriage or that they were practicing homosexuals. The media did not reveal that public figures, including presidents, were having extramarital affairs. Even Franklin D. Roosevelt's obvious physical handicap was hidden. We were never permitted to see him in anything but a sitting or standing position. Things were more orderly on the outside so that our chaos on the inside could be more easily contained.

But under the appearances, as we now know, things were often something other. Yet, outwardly, order prevailed. Ronald Reagan's appeal may have been solidified early in his first term when he broke the air traffic controllers' strike. For the increasing number of people dependent upon air travel for their economic survival, he was the leader of order over chaos. He took the dare against possible hazards to safety and pulled it off. Someone was in charge—in control. Such reassurance helps us to feel more in control—of our lives and, particularly, of our own latent inner chaos.

But the potential for this chaos is still there. Meaning is still under siege. Under our facade of control, the disorder of our conflicting passions continues to feed our anxiety. Should it escalate, we may be plunged once again into despair. Whether or not we are religious in the biblical sense, we will then cry out, "My God—my meaning—my purpose—why have you forsaken me!"

The healing for this despair, including the anxiety implicit in it, will not be found by returning to a past that does not take into account the direction in which we have moved. We need to look to a future in which God will reveal to us his good news for our particular time.

CHAPTER 3
How Ageism Complicates the Aging Process

When he was 80 years old, American writer and critic Malcolm Cowley wrote an article for *Life* magazine which he later expanded into the book *The View from Eighty* (Viking Press, 1980). Cowley believes most of the literature on the subject of the older years is written in too positive a vein largely because its authors are in their later fifties and early sixties when they write, a time when most of them lack genuine knowledge and are trying to be cheerful about what is ahead. As one who is there, Cowley emphasizes the changes that take place in one's self-image because of the messages one receives.

Some of these messages come from our aging bodies, which limit not only our physical activity but also our thinking about ourselves. But more insistent and devastating than these body messages are the messages we receive from other people. "We start by growing old in other people's eyes," Cowley says, "and then slowly we come to share their judgment," which even if meted out in kindness has a cruel effect. He describes, as a personal experience of this transfer of messages, the time a young woman got up and offered him her seat on a crowded bus. "Can't I even stand up? I thought as I thanked her and declined the seat." But the second time he "gratefully accepted" the offer, though with "a sense of having diminished myself" (*The View from Eighty,* pp. 5–6).

Ageist Myths and Discriminations

The fact that the messages we get from others regarding our aging are so decisive in shaping our own attitudes is compounded in its devastating effect when these messages are distorted by ageist myths and discriminations. These myths and discriminations are not only widespread in our culture but also are not questioned by most of us. Instead, we take them for granted. This, of course, affects our sensitivity—or lack of it.

Ageism is as discriminatory as racism and sexism, only we have been slower to recognize it as such. In fact, it is rarely mentioned when discriminatory practices are discussed. Reflecting on his ministry, a Christian pastor wrote, "I remember my own hedging on racial and women's issues—long after I knew in my heart that our behavior in the church was shameful in both areas." What about his hedging on ageism? On the church's ageist policies? I'm sure that this particular discrimination never entered his head. Yet we as a culture are as steeped in ageist bias as we have been and in many ways still are in racist and sexist biases.

In all probability there was no discriminatory attitude on the part of the young woman who offered Cowley her seat. She was being kind. Yet she probably was also totally insensitive to the effect her offer had on him. My seminary class in the Ministry with the Aged is almost like a sensitivity seminar for many of the students. In their evaluations at the conclusion of the course they frequently acknowledge that they had not previously been aware of the ageist slurs, biases, and discriminatory practices that were occurring in their midst. Once their eyes were opened, they were amazed at how entrenched we as a society are in our ageist attitudes.

These ageisms are even accepted by the aged themselves. I was housed in a home for the aged during a speaking engagement because of its convenient location.

I not only slept there but also ate my meals at my assigned seat with the residents. Each of us had our own cloth napkin, which was used from one meal to the next. Being unaware of the arrangement, I unintentionally picked up the napkin that belonged to the person seated next to me. He reminded me that using the same napkin was a sanitary measure. Then he said with discernible bitterness, "We all have a mild case of leprosy here": Like the biblical leprosy, old age was a disease which made one a social outcast.

Contrary to other discriminations, such as those of sex and race, ageist discrimination affects everyone who lives long enough. The irony is that not only are more people living longer today but the discrimination practiced against the elderly has its ripple effect much earlier. Witness those who find themselves out of work in their fifties! As a society, we so fear the leprosy of old age that we begin to safeguard ourselves against it decades ahead of time.

The entrance into the older years is symbolized by retirement. Retirements based on years of service, such as those associated with military or civil service, are of course excepted. Rather, it is those retirements that are mandatory because of chronological age which for most workplaces is now permitted by law only at age 70. However, since pressure is often applied to encourage employees to retire earlier than this, the traditional age of 65 remains a significant milestone for many. Forced or harassed retirement is symbolic for the onset of the "disease of old age" because it means one is no longer wanted in the working world—the marketplace where life in our society has its focus.

This ejection from the workaday world has traditionally been harder on men than on women. Women who did not work outside the home never retired from their assumed roles, except in mid-life, when the care for young children came to an end. If women survived this "retirement," they were in good shape for the rest of their lives. Even now, when most women work outside the home in addition to their homemaking role, they may not be as locked into their jobs as expressions of their worth as are men, perhaps because of these other roles. They still are often more involved in other areas of life than are men. The fact that women tend to have less creative and less challenging jobs may also account for this difference.

When men retire, it seems, they retire from more than a job. They retire from their source of meaning and purpose and worth. Even the social life of men tends to center at the job. This is why many men on retiring speak about coming back to the workplace frequently to visit. If they do so, they find it is not the same, and they no longer have a place. So the frequent trips back seldom materialize.

Because the incidence of sickness and death rises dramatically after retirement, it is puzzling to me that forced retirement has not been seen as at least one possible contribution to the earlier ages of death for men in our society. If women are by and large spared this trauma, they are thus better prepared for the changes to come in later years.

Rejection Hard to Take

Rejection is always hard to take. It is harder to take, however, when it comes to us for the first time in our later years. Most of us are simply not prepared for rejection by previous experience, so it is difficult even to anticipate. For some, this rejection comes on gradually, and for others it hits home suddenly. My mother was 83 years old before—as far as anyone knew—she realized she was supposed to be old. She discovered this when she was hospitalized for pneumonia, and she shared the experience with me very somberly. "They tell me here that I am old," she said. I could see the effect this labeling had on her spirit. Pneumonia used to be called the old folks' friend because it mercifully brought their death, but with antibiotics this has radically changed. My mother should have recovered, according to her physician. But she didn't. Perhaps had she not been stigmatized when she was especially vulnerable, the antibiotics might have had a better chance.

How had my mother escaped this label for so long? Obviously she had had good health. But in addition she was still doing what she had always been doing—home-making and church work. She had never retired.

I have a friend who made this discovery much earlier. He had always thought of himself in terms associated in our society with the young—energetic, involved, alert, competent, "on the way up." But through circumstances over which he had little control he found himself without a job in his vulnerable years. Supported by his mental image of himself, he assumed he would soon find something even better than before, particularly with his many years of experience. But he ran into ageism. At first it didn't sink in. After a few more interviews, however, he was stunned into believing it. "I'm running into this age business," he said. "When I say I'm sixty-two the atmo-sphere of the interview suddenly changes. Even though people continue to be polite, I can sense it's all over!" His countenance showed his sagging spirit. For the first time in the job market he was up against something he felt helpless to combat.

Some people are not hit with the reality of their rejection until after retirement. There is a kind of romanticism attached to retirement. Now they will be able to do as they like: stay in bed in the morning, take a nap in the afternoon, go on a trip, play golf whenever they feel like it, fish, visit the children. But like all romantic visions this one also has difficulty enduring the test of reality and time. John C. Bennett, retired professor of theology, who spoke recently in a lectureship at my seminary in his early eighties, put it well: "After one has had enough of the anticipated satisfaction of leisure, having no place to go regularly away from home, the attraction of retirement may pall" (William M. Clements, ed., *Ministry with the Aging*, p. 143; Harper & Row, 1981).

Forced retirement is itself a mark of rejection. One is ominously aware as the years continue that on a certain date one will be evicted—rejected—by the very organization or institution within which one now plays some significant role. There may of course be a party or even a gold watch to help take away the sting, but this hardly compensates for what is being taken away. Archibald Cox, the former Watergate prosecutor, commented, after he was required to retire at age 70 as a professor at the Harvard Law School, "I am presumed to be senile" (*Time*, April 4, 1984, p. 65).

Yet Cox *continues* as president of Common Cause and, since his retirement, has testified before congressional committees in his lobbying role. What about those who do not have a cause—some significant work to do—after forced retirement? There are far more people in this situation than in situations like that of Archibald Cox. Bennett is unequivocal in his opposition to forced retirement. "Certainly the contributions of experienced and able people should not be recklessly discarded as is often the case today: arbitrary absolutes about retirement age should be abandoned" (*Ministry with the Aging*, p. 143).

Noted economist John Kenneth Galbraith provides a needed distinction between "work" and "real work." Real work is what one does for a living. It may require a skill but it lacks creative challenge. It is hard, or tedious, or physically or mentally exhausting, often boring, and often dead-end. Even when it entails heavy responsibilities and involves leadership, it is often for bosses and owners who provide little if any affirmation and even less job security. "They so labor because they are paid," says Galbraith. "They would not dream of doing it otherwise." The other kind of work should not be called work at all. While people are paid for it, they do it because they enjoy it, even love doing it. This kind of work is often called a career. It satisfies creative energies as well as values and ideals. The work may have its routine and frustrating features, but the overall tenor is one of excitement and challenge.

For those who do real work, retirement—if adequately supported—says Galbraith, "is a human right." For those who do what is fraudulently called work, the right of retirement should exist, he says, "but the basic right should be that of continued employment. There should be no arbitrary retirement age."

Galbraith held the latter kind of job as a teacher of economics. Obviously, retirement had no appeal for him. Yet he hesitated to challenge the requirement that he leave when he reached 70, and he is now retired from his teaching position. Forced retirement is unnecessary for real work; people will usually choose it as a way of having a living without having to continue to work for it. Forced retirement is wrong for those whose work is not really work, because they are usually well able to continue after the age of 70. Some, of course, may not be. A set retirement age "is really a design for avoiding difficult individual judgments by imposing a harsh arbitrary rule on all." Galbraith gives short shrift to the argument that forced retirement opens the job to younger people who otherwise might be held up in their careers by older workers. "We should not accept the common argument that forced retirement is necessary to make room for younger newcomers; there is no fixed limit on the number of employable men and women in the economy. The answer here— the only answer—is to have an economy and polity that have need and room for all" ("When Work Isn't Work," *Parade* magazine, Feb. 10, 1985, pp. 10–11).

Older people, particularly when they are retired and hold no responsible position in society, are usually taken less seriously than those who are younger and still in the work force. Without a job, a community responsibility, they have no place. When people have no place they have no status, no authority, and little worth. Their lack of position provides little justification for others to listen to them except as a tolerant alternative to rudeness. Malcolm Cowley again speaks from experience. "Those who are older are made to feel that they no longer have a function in the community. Their families and neighbors don't ask them for advice, don't really listen when they speak, don't call on them for efforts" (*The View from Eighty,* p. 16). It is difficult not to accept this rejection by society and simply give up.

The older person who is physically incapacitated by age is taken even less seriously. The nursing home patient, for example, may be considered by well-meaning staff as an amusing child. Carobeth Laird had her first book published when she was 80 and her second a year or so later. She was working on two other books when she became physically incapacitated and had to enter a nursing home. This experience gave rise to another book, *Limbo,* an ominous title for her account of her experience in the home, which she described as "neither the best nor the worst of nursing homes—not horrible, just dehumanizing." She fought a losing battle to maintain some independence. She was not permitted telephone calls, and her editor finally got through to her only by conferring on her the title of Professor Laird and demanding that she be called to the phone. She was placed with patients who were severely incapacitated mentally, and she had to fight for her sanity by reading whatever she could get from the very limited nursing home library. "If I mentioned anything about my life or my books, the aides merely humored me with their condescending 'yes, dear, no, dear!' There was no respect for a person's dignity" (Carobeth Laird, "An Old Woman Who Dreams—and Writes Books," *Parade* magazine, July 30, 1978, p. 7).

While there are many horror stories about life in nursing homes, there are also many uplifting stories of homes that try to provide the dignity to their patients that Mrs. Laird missed. Yet the very place that older people have in our culture, particularly when made more dependent by physical infirmities, makes it difficult for both staff and patients to provide an atmosphere of genuine rather than contrived dignity. And the depleted self-image of an older person can frustrate the effort as much as the unconscious patronizing of the staff.

Events Interpreted by Age

Anything that happens to older people that is negative we tend to view in light of their age. Younger people can forget, and it is laughed off. But if older people forget, it is a sign of their deteriorating brain. Dr. Spock says he is fastidiously careful about eliminating food stains on his clothes. While he might get away with these in his earlier years, he knows such spots will be interpreted in his eighties as indicators of encroaching debilitation.

But the most threatening of such ageist interpretations concerns the automobile. When older people have an automobile accident they know they are in danger of losing their driver's license. When an elderly friend had this happen to him he lost more than his license—he lost his self-confidence. To understand this we need only recognize the place the automobile holds in our society. It is the American adult's security blanket. Our independence, our sense of control, ultimately our identity reside in our car. We lose all these as a rider on a bus. Mass transit in the United States is up against more than its expensiveness. For many people the car is tied up with their sense of meaning. This becomes even more so as one ages.

In a home for the aged that I visited, the staff shared with me an incident that had recently stirred up some excitement. Around midnight the night attendants became curious and then alarmed by the continuing sound of a running motor in the parking lot. Somebody was out there, but who and why? Finally they called the police. When the police arrived and checked on the motorist, there was none—only an empty car with the motor running. They traced the license number and discovered that the car belonged to a resident of the home. While this resident rarely drove his car, because he had few places to go, he would regularly start the motor and let it run awhile. This time he had forgotten to turn it off. Running the motor when a car is rarely used is a nuisance for most people. For this man it was part of a structure of activities that reassured him that he still had his independence, his control, his identity.

Ageist Slurs

Besides racist and sexist slurs, concerning which we have been sensitized, we have also ageist slurs. Labels like "little old lady" and "senile old man" too often go unchallenged. I have even heard professional caregivers disdainfully refer to their work as "holding little old ladies' hands." To select as identification marks of the aged the unfortunate malady of osteoporosis, or decreasing of bone mass in elderly women, and the mental deterioration that may afflict some older persons for any number of reasons, is to indulge in slurs. Yet these as well as others too often go unchallenged.

I am particularly bothered by the ageist slurs that appear regularly in the media. Newspaper columnists are cases in point. Usually they are subtle about it. "Older women, in their sixties and seventies, women set in their ways," wrote one such columnist in my local newspaper. This reference is an ageist myth as well as a slur. Another columnist in the same paper criticized the Lebanon policy of President Reagan by reasonably dealing with the issues. Yet he could not resist taking advantage of Reagan's chronological age vulnerability by calling him an "old man." The use of this derogatory appellation would indicate that we haven't progressed much since the name-calling days of Senator Joseph McCarthy, who attacked Senator Charles Tobey as senile because the 73-year-old Tobey was leading the opposition to McCarthy's activities in the Senate.

A national syndicated columnist was not quite so blatant. In expressing his criticism of governmental inaction he singled out adversaries Ronald Reagan and Tip O'Neill, referring to them as "a couple of septuagenarians," a form of name-calling when none of the other senators to whom he referred were described by their age bracket. When I wrote to him to protest this ageist slur, he said he meant nothing derogatory in using the term. Rather, he said, he used it to indicate that persons in that age bracket are more rigid and hence less flexible to make fresh decisions. The irony was that he seemed not to recognize the ageist myth in his own explanation. There is obviously a need for sensitization regarding ageist myths and slurs so that people at least recognize them when confronted with them.

Focus at the Workplace

Ageist discrimination can be seen most clearly at the workplace. Older employees or job applicants are often in for a hazardous time. A policeman was forced to retire from the Detroit Police Department because he had reached the age of 63. He sued, and the department was forced to take him back until age 70. His comment on being reinstated was that he was going to do all that he could to advance in the department in the years remaining to him.

Age discrimination court cases were rare only a decade ago. They now have become a major area of litigation. A typical case is that of Miriam Geller. She was 55 when, as a teacher with eleven years of experience, she began a new teaching job in an elementary school. After only the second week on the job she was told she was being replaced—by a 27-year-old woman with only three years of experience. Said Geller, "While I've never been much of an activist before, I was angry enough about this that I wanted to do something about it" (*St. Paul Pioneer Press*, Nov. 15, 1981, p. 6).

The school system contended—as is usually the case—that it was not discriminating against older teachers but had adopted a cost-cutting policy of not hiring teachers with more than six years of experience. Geller's lawyer was able to show that such a policy obviously excluded the older job applicant. She won the case and the school board was forced not only to reinstate her but to abandon its ageist hiring policy.

As ageist discrimination cases increase, so also do the subtleties in ageist hiring policies. Since application forms are not permitted to ask about age, employers instead schedule an interview in which the applicant is asked to give the date of his or her high school graduation. In this way, by visual appearance and by confirming high school graduation date, older applicants are screened out, while being told only that the job is not available to someone with his or her credentials.

Geller had to wait six years for her case to be settled, not an uncommon situation in our legal system. During this time she kept looking for a job and found many people in the same age bind as she—"people past 40." But they seemed resigned to their fate. "That's the way it is!" Unlike Geller, they were giving in rather than fighting back.

As we have seen, ageist discrimination is hard to prove because no employer is going to own up to it. Rather,

subtle substitute issues are used. Yet ageist discriminations are no more difficult to prove than are racist and
sexist discriminations. Discriminators rarely confess
since they rarely repent. Instead, they deny it or defend
themselves on some other basis.

While we as Christians acknowledge that ageist discrimination is wrong, the fact is that the Christian church
as an institution is *as* ageist and sometimes even *more*
ageist than other institutions. Perhaps this should not
surprise us; the same thing has been said of the church
regarding its racism and sexism. It is when the government begins to act against discriminatory practices that
the church as an institution begins to change its ways.
Although the government has begun to act against ageist
discrimination by moving the compulsory retirement age
from 65 to 70, for example, the church has barely begun
to change its discriminatory practices.

In metropolitan areas, churches are concentrated
where older people are less likely to live: in the suburbs.
Where they are more likely to live, in the central city,
churches are fewer and poorer. The trend of young
adults moving back into cities in gentrification projects
may alter this to some extent, but as yet this has not
shown itself in the makeup of most inner-city congregations.

Where churches are most blatantly ageist is in the
calling of clergy. Congregations tend to want younger
pastors who can "work well with youth." Yet there is no
evidence that age is a deciding factor in the effectiveness
of a youth ministry. In this, as in other ministries, the
individual pastor makes the difference. In fact, young
people are often very close to their grandparents—closer
at times than to their parents. Even congregations are
becoming careful now not to mention age in selecting a
pastor. But one pastor with whom I visited was told by the
committee who had interviewed him that despite his
good qualifications they believed that "their congrega-

tion required a younger person as pastor." "Don't they know," he said, "that I am in my prime?"

Studies show that this pastor was correct—not just about the ministry but also about other jobs and careers. These studies show that older workers not only bring to their jobs a wealth of knowledge and skills but also have fewer short-term illnesses and absences and are more stable than younger workers, who may still be making career decisions. This is the opinion of Jerome M. Roscow of the Work in America Institute and a former assistant secretary of labor. Because older workers have accrued more benefits, in the short run it is cheaper for businesses to terminate them. But it is to their long-run interest to retain older workers because of the caliber and steadiness of their work. As the baby boom generation moves into the over-fifty group, there may well be a shortage of young workers. Realizing this, some companies are doing some strategic planning in this regard, such as the retraining of older workers for new tasks as well as recalling former employees from retirement.

Ageism Fails to Recognize Differences

Ageism is discriminatory because it fails to recognize differences among older people. There are older people who may be living primarily in the past, who are resting on past laurels, and who have ceased to grow either in their job or as persons. "Those of us in university life," says Galbraith, "have often noticed that senility frequently afflicts a scholar immediately after achieving tenure." On the other hand there are those who at the same age are at the cutting edge of their vocation, are enthusiastically involved in life and in their job. To lump these two different kinds of older people together because they share a common chronological age is highly discriminatory.

This difference among people in their personal and

mental activities reflects a similar difference in their physical functioning. Dr. Alvin Smith, chief oncologist at Halifax Hospital in Daytona Beach, Florida, estimates that 85 percent of the diseases occur in 15 percent of the people. "Chronological age," he said, "means nothing. It is the physiological age that counts. Some seem ninety at sixty while others seem sixty at ninety" (Personal interview, Jan. 18, 1985).

Ageist discrimination is based on prioritizing quantity of years over quality of years. Yet in our own experience as humans it is obviously quality of time that is the more important criterion. In biblical chronology, for example, what are Methuselah's 969 years compared to Jesus' 33 years? In our own modern era what did John XXIII's few years as pope contribute to this papacy? Those who chose him for this position when he was 77 may well have had a caretaking role in mind, a holding job for a brief transitional period. His papacy was brief and it was also transitional, but not in the way that one might have thought. John had other things in mind. He pursued change as rapidly and perhaps more wisely than many a younger man. Fortunately there was no arbitrary retirement of cardinals at age 70!

At the other end of the age spectrum, Jesus also had only a brief time for his ministry. But the briefness had little to do with the change in the world that he accomplished. "Jesus, when he began his ministry, was about thirty years of age" (Luke 3:23). Luke could say this because thirty was the age of majority at that time, which kept Jesus from beginning his ministry earlier. This of course can be looked at as ageist discrimination at the other end of the age spectrum. Other cultures, as we shall note further, are often the reverse of us in ageist discrimination. Elihu, the fourth counselor in the book of Job, had to hold his peace while the others spoke with Job, because he was the youngest. When he finally got his turn, the wait had not only angered him but *soured* him on the "wisdom of the aged." "I am young in years and you are aged. . . . I said, 'Let days speak, and many years teach wisdom.' But it is the spirit in a man, the breath of the Almighty, that makes him understand. It is not the old that are wise, nor the aged that understand what is right" (Job 32:6–9). Søren Kierkegaard was only 42 when he died, and he felt similarly about the aged. "Why, I wonder," he said, "did Socrates love youth, if it was not because he knew man" (*Sickness Unto Death*, p. 59). For in aging one can go from something one had in youth and never again be as attuned to spiritual reality.

Like all discriminatory practices, ageism depends on generalizations and thereby loses sight of the individual. The chronology of years supersedes the quality of those years, and the result is a tragic loss for the human community.

CHAPTER 4
Becoming Older
Rather than Old

The word "old" has a stigma attached to it in our culture. It places one in a group that is relegated to the sidelines—out of it, as far as where the action is. In a recent sabbatical project I submitted a questionnaire to 1,300 clergy to ascertain their attitude toward themselves and their occupation. One of the variables to which they were to respond with varying degrees of agreement or disagreement was, "I am getting old."

How would you respond to this variable? I found many people were confused by it. "How can this be a variable," they would ask, "since if you are getting old, you *are*?" I explained that if this were true there would have to be a consensus on what age is considered *old,* and there is none. The only nonvariable would be, "I am getting older." In contrast to *older,* old is largely an attitude—an interpretation of *older*—picked up from our culture and applied to oneself or others at varying ages.

In other cultures, especially Third World cultures, there is no such stigma to "old." In fact, there is an honor attributed to the word. Instead of being out of it, one is entering "into it." Although I was aware of this difference, it was brought forcefully home to me in my seminary class in "Ministry with the Aged" in which a student from Nigeria simply could not comprehend why anyone would fear growing old. "In my country," he said, "this is what we look forward to." Mid-life crisis was a thoroughly new term to him. What could be meant by a crisis in mid-life? Growing old? For Nigerians this is an upward, not a downward, trek in time. Your only hope is that you will live long enough to arrive. Then you will reap the reward of your years—the added prestige in the community that can come only at this time of life. Old age in Nigeria is the desired destination of one's life journey. This is obviously a different context from ours within which to view the process and symptoms of aging.

The Key Is How One Interprets

The key to improvement of life in the later years is a positive interpretation of the passage into these years. In our culture the interpretation is negative, and so we are programmed to become *old* rather than *older*. Such programming results from a conspiracy in which most of us are involved.

A central factor in this programming is our ageist medical practices. What older people hear repeatedly from their physician is "you can expect these health problems at your age." What we expect we may also program. Our mental attitude has a lot to do with what "happens" to us. This negative programming can begin early. I was only 36 years old when I first heard it. I had developed bursitis in my shoulder from playing volley-ball. After asking my age, the orthopedic physician informed me that I could begin to expect these ailments as I entered mid-life. Fortunately I did not believe him. Now, quite a bit beyond 36, I have not had bursitis in my shoulder for years, even though I am still as active.

Unfortunately, the medical advice that many older people receive is to learn to live with their disabilities—to adapt to the inevitable. Using a cane or taking pain-reducing medication may help in this adaptation. This may be the best advice and assistance that can be given. It also may keep us from considering other ways to alleviate the situation. The role of nutrition and exercise, for example, in both preventing and alleviating debilitating illnesses usually associated with old age, has only recently been recognized by the medical profession. Where orthodox medical practice is inadequate, some people have found help in chiropractic. Some physicians recommend this course to patients they believe might profit from it. Though one does not understand why something helps, it may still help. Even the placebo should not be discounted as a placebo if it is instrumental in healing. The power of our beliefs on our bodies can be amazing.

When our culture's interpretation of old age is the context within which the physician interprets the ailments of the elderly, the result too often is an inadequate medical diagnosis. Were the person to have the same ailment twenty or thirty years earlier, the diagnostic approach may be considerably more thorough. Unfortunately, if the diagnosis is inadequate, the treatment is likely to be also. The lamentable physical condition of some elderly people may result, at least partially, from the accumulation of such medical neglect. Iatrogenic illnesses—resulting from medical treatment—are caused by physicians' omissions as well as commissions.

Fortunately, there have always been many physicians who were not taken in by ageist bias and who treated each elderly person as an individual whose symptoms might reveal correctable problems. Fortunately also, this ageist bias in diagnosis and treatment is being increasingly recognized by the medical profession. There are doctors who specialize in geriatrics. But this is only a beginning. Every physician needs to be a geriatrics specialist, because the majority of the patients of most physicians are in this age bracket.

Few ailments are the automatic result of aging. Yet when people are told by medical authorities that they can expect such ailments as they age, the effect is similar to that of a placebo, except in the opposite direction. We program ourselves to age *badly*. When physicians use the term "degeneracy" with their patients in describing changes in the body—as has been done with me on more than one occasion—these patients may begin not only to see themselves as degenerating but also to feel this way as well.

With the continued debates in Congress over the cost of medical care and, in particular, Medicare, we need to remind ourselves that the health needs of the aged are going to be solved not only by making medical care more available to them financially but also by improving the medical care they receive. In fact, a total health care program for the aged would begin far earlier, with a wellness program for mind and body, so that *less* rather than more medical care is needed.

The conspiracy in negative programming for aging includes also the elderly themselves. Physical ailments can become the focus of older people's concerns when their lives lack a focus otherwise. Some older people need their ailments to fill a vacuum in their lives; others need them to distract their attention from the hard-to-face realities of what has happened to them as "old folks." When I stayed at the home for the aged I was impressed by the attention that physical ailments received in the conversations in which I engaged the residents. But as I became aware of the limited span of interests in which their lives were lived in that home, I had difficulty ascertaining what might replace ailments as a focus for concern.

Once ailments become the major focus, taking medication is part and parcel of this preoccupation. So the physician is pressured by the elderly residents to provide this medication. We are creatures of habit and need the help of others to support our habits. Ours is an addictive culture. We seek quick even if temporary relief from suffering and are resistant to doing what needs to be done to become more genuinely healthy. Physicians have at times, particularly in the past, given way to this addiction. These drugs require prescriptions. These drugs became a problem not because they cannot be helpful—they can—but because people become addicted to them, psychologically at least, as a means of coping with their life rather than using them as transitional help in difficult situations. The elderly are no exception to this trend. What these elderly really need is a vision, a purpose, a meaning for living. Lacking a place in society, they turn in on themselves—on their bodies.

Downhill All the Way

When we are programmed to see the aging process as "downhill all the way," we lose the vision of health and are left with only the forebodings of illness. This perspective in which we view our life and future is hard on our sense of meaning and purpose because it is hard on our self-esteem. Worthlessness, uselessness, purposelessness, and meaninglessness all go together. They are all ingredients in the culmination of despair. The comparatively high suicide rate among the elderly is caused at least in part by this bleak perspective of the future of aging.

Those who refuse to buy into this negative perspective are the healthier among us. A film on aging produced by Augsburg Publishing House entitled *Years of Vitality,* presented theologian Joseph Sittler and Congressman Claude Pepper, among others. Sittler, in his early eighties, said he was actually a poor person to interview on this question because he had not given it much thought. "I've been too involved with the things I'm doing to realize that I am aging," he said. Pepper, in his mid-eighties, the chairperson of the House of Representatives Committee on Aging, said that he gets up in the morning excited about the things he needs to do that day—as well as the next. "If I didn't have this responsibility," he said, "I'm sure I would deteriorate very quickly."

Twenty-five years ago, when he was 72, attorney John A. Sibley was asked by the Georgia State Legislature to head up a commission to decide what to do with Georgia public schools in light of the U.S. Supreme Court's decision to put an end to school segregation. After two months of hearings on this highly charged issue, the commission recommended integrating the public schools rather than closing them. Today, at 97, Sibley goes each day to his office in an Atlanta bank of which he is honorary chairperson of the board and has appointments from 11 A.M. to 4 P.M. People drop in for advice or just to chat. His particular challenge today is a lawsuit he has filed on behalf of farmers that their property be taxed for its value as a farm and not for its potential value as a site for development. When asked why he has pursued so many activities for so many years, Sibley answered, "I've seen people have a single interest in life, and their usefulness dried up and they're done for after the single interest is gone. I'd like to put myself in a different class. I feel like your *usefulness* is not exhausted if you have a number of interests" (Robert M. Press, "Papa's Kindness and Ability Hold Kin and Community Together," *Christian Science Monitor,* May 5, 1985, p. 7).

In contrast to Sibley's perspective on living, our patronizing culture encourages the "retirement" of the elderly from usefulness and thus is also a conspirator in the negative programming for aging. A student calling on an elderly person in a hospital reflected this cultural prejudice. The patient was lonely, but instead of listening to an expression of this loneliness, the student found the first convenient opportunity to terminate the visit by saying, "I'll let you rest now."

What older people do not need in the daytime, unless they are seriously ill, which was not the case in this instance, is *rest.* Rest is a symbol for retirement, uninvolvement, "off to the side." What older people need, what all of us need during the daytime, is *stimulation*. Even negative stimulation—irritation, anger—is better for physical, mental, and spiritual health than no stimulation at all. The "nice" private room, with the shades drawn to keep out the brightness of daylight and the door shut to screen out the noises from the hallway, becomes a prolepsis of a tomb. Bright light, noise, even irritable noise, and involvement in the life of the corridors are encouragements for healing—for life.

I ask my students to choose a person who models for them growing older meaningfully. One young man chose his grandfather, who at 90 has strong convictions, a clear mind, and a healthy body. He told the class about his grandfather's lifelong concern for good nutrition and his lack of reticence in encouraging others in the family to follow his example. Our class was impressed not only by his wisdom—he was certainly ahead of his time—but also by the way he himself at 90 was evidence for the value of his life-style.

Yet the student's own family was not that impressed. His children say, "Oh, that's Grandpa!" and dismiss what he has to say. Grandpa was easily dismissed either because he is old or because what he says has become an old tape or both. Yet he could have provided a lot of sensible advice for his children and grandchildren in regard to their own aging. His value as a model was not recognized by those most in position to profit from it. Yet Grandfather did not buy their patronizing dismissal of him. He kept affirming himself. And the student for the first time realized what was happening in his family and was appalled, not only by the obvious ageist attitude but by the folly of resisting the grandfather's counsel.

I've seen this same dismissal of the elderly even in programs on aging itself. At one that I attended, the only really elderly person present had to *ask* for the floor. "I'd like to give a testimony," he said. "To grow older meaningfully you need to have *plans*. I'm only thirteen years from a hundred, but I have plans. I talked to a young man this week and asked him about his plans. He said, 'I don't have any.' *He's* old, I'm not." Since his retirement at 70, this man has taught in New Guinea and India, and has visited China several times, and is now planning another trip abroad.

Can you imagine a forum on racial issues or women's issues conducted only by whites or by men, where the blacks or women present had to *ask* to speak? How many older people have the temerity to resist this exclusion and ask for the floor? Fortunately this man did. He gave the most sensible comment of the day.

If John Sibley is right that our usefulness won't end if we keep active, then a culture that tries to persuade its elderly *not* to be active but to rest is conspiring against their usefulness. Religiously speaking, this amounts to placing cultural obstacles in the way of the divine calling.

Following his conversation with Jimmy Carter about the ex-President's work at the Carter Center—where world leaders gather to work on problems that desperately need solutions—*Christian Century* editor James Wall said, "A phrase hit me as he talked: service to others. Jimmy Carter is using his prestige as a former President to do precisely what he learned was his duty as a small boy in his Plains Baptist church. We have been put on earth *to serve others*. . . . Because one has been born again, saved, redeemed, given a gift (take your pick) one *must* find a way to serve others" (James Wall, "Jimmy Carter, Religion and Public Service," *Christian Century*, May 8, 1985, p. 459).

One's divine calling to be useful—to serve others—does not cease as one becomes older. It may require adaptations to be carried out, but it must continue to be the focus for living if we are to continue to be *human* in the Christian understanding of that term. Consequently, the patronizing persuasion to rest—to take it easy, to retire, to stay to the side, to watch others do it—is dehumanizing.

The Value of Experience

The wisdom that comes from living, from utilizing the experiences of time, is not valued by our culture. Rather, we value the wisdom that comes from scientific research. In the matter of aging we value the information given by those who do the studies on aging rather than the wisdom of the aged themselves. We value the knowledge that is accredited by academic degrees rather than that which comes from the process of living. The instance of the school that limited its teaching applicants to those with no more than six years of experience is a case in point. They did so to cut costs; experienced teachers cost more. Obviously the school board didn't think they were worth it, didn't value experience as a basis for good teaching. Yet wisdom is needed to accompany knowledge and direct its use.

A man recognized for his wisdom in the business world was interviewed by a cub reporter. "What is the secret to your success?" he asked. "Two words," said the business-man. "Right decisions." "How does one learn to make right decisions?" asked the reporter. "One word," said the tycoon. "Experience." "And how does one get this experience?" asked the reporter. "Two words," the tycoon said. "Wrong decisions."

The "right decisions" that characterize wisdom do not come automatically with the aging process. Some *never* learn. According to 2 Timothy such persons are like Jannes and Jambres, the reputed names of the Egyptian magicians at Pharaoh's court who tried to prevent the liberation of the Hebrews by duplicating the "magic" of Aaron's rod that turned to a serpent, only to have their serpents devoured by Aaron's rod (Ex. 7:5–18). These men "will listen to anybody and can never arrive at a knowledge of the truth" (2 Tim. 3:7). So, says 2 Timothy, were some in the church of that day. "As Jannes and Jambres opposed Moses, so these men also oppose" (v. 8). But the writer is sure they will not delude people forever. "Their folly will be plain to all, as was that of those two men" (v. 9).

The key to experience being converted into wisdom is *repentance*. If we can face up to our mistakes, blunders, and sins—as the businessman said, our "wrong decisions"—we are more likely to profit from the experience. We are all entitled to make our own mistakes. We who have learned the hard way try to protect those who are younger by giving them our advice to save them the pain. Yet it is through the pain—repentance, contrition—that one really *learns*.

A young assistant pastor lamented that his senior pastor was so wise that he knew whether or not something would work because of his vast experience. "When I suggest something that I might do regarding certain parish needs, my pastor says, 'I can save you the trouble. I tried it several times and it doesn't work.' What I really want from him is the freedom to make my *own* mistakes."

We parents have the difficult challenge of gradually releasing our teenage children to adult responsibilities. It is difficult because we don't want them "to go through what we went through." We want them to profit from *our* experience so they won't have to learn from *theirs*. Yet in our wiser moments we know that this is not the way it works. We have to take the risk of letting our children go and suffer with them in their pains over their own "wrong decisions"—or the wrong decisions of others in regard to them. The process of leaving father and mother is a major passage in aging. It is the way of becoming adult and gaining through experience the wisdom needed to direct our knowledge. Growing older meaningfully begins early in one's life.

Unlike the senior pastor who desired to use his

experience to *protect* the younger generation from making mistakes, some older persons dwell on past achievements in order to *gain the respect* of the younger generation. They yearn to be recognized in their later years, and bragging about their past seems the only recourse open to them. This apparent vanity, says Malcolm Cowley, is one of the vices of aging. Since their future is bleak, older people turn to the time when they *had* recognition or at least in retrospect it seems they did. This vanity is easily understood, and Cowley believes it should also be easily condoned.

He recalled the time when he was a guest for dinner when the host, an aged athlete-no-longer, tried to find his athletic letter sweater to show to his guests. "Oh, that old thing," his wife said. "The moths got into it and I threw it away." The former athlete sulked, and the guests went home early (*The View from Eighty*, p. 11).

Sometimes this yearning to be recognized appears only as an innocent boast. The "good parent" telling how *she* handled things in *her* family, the "wise foreman" sharing how *he* controlled *his* shop, the "dependable secretary" telling about *her* long hours of overtime in devotion to *her* boss, the "church deacon" who braved *his* pastor's intimidation and spoke *his* mind. These "innocent boasts" recur frequently in the conversations of some elderly people.

Cowley quotes Cicero's *De Senectute:* "What is more charming than an old age surrounded by the enthusiasm of youth! . . . Attentions which seem trivial and conventional are marks of honor—the morning call, being sought after, precedence, having people rise for you, being escorted to and from the forum. . . . What pleasures of the body can be compared to the prerogatives of influence?" Cowley agrees. "To be admired and praised, especially by the young, is an autumnal pleasure enjoyed by the lucky ones (who are not always the most deserving)" (*View from Eighty*, p. 12).

What about the unlucky ones—even those who may be deserving? It's hard to be without the "prerogatives of influence," particularly when one has had them in the past. This "search for honors is a harmless passion," Cowley contends, even though the boasting gets tedious. Since "honors cost little, why shouldn't the very old have more than their share of them?" (*View from Eighty,* p. 11).

This vanity in seeking recognition from the younger generation may also indicate a lifelong penchant for boasting that has only become "more so" with age. People who in mid-life downplay their mistakes and avoid facing their sins reveal an exaggerated tendency to have to be *right*. They gain their respect by making themselves the heroes or heroines of all of their stories. With their decline in influence in the later years, this tendency grows worse as they desperately try the only way they have known to gain or regain respect.

Repentance as the Key to Wisdom

Again, the key to wisdom is repentance. Repentance is not simply admitting when we are wrong, or confessing our sins, but doing so in *hope*. According to the gospel, we are not judged by our mistakes, failures, or sins, so we are freed from the fear of rejection to face them honestly. Then we can grow in our personal resources through the passages of life. By the same token we do not have to defend ourselves or project an image of competence in order to ward off would-be critics. We do not have to "have it all together," either in our past or in our present, to gain respect.

Repentance as a way of life is possible when the gospel is the basis for this way of life. There is forgiveness, there is grace, there is justification apart from our accomplishments. So there is freedom to risk—to grow. Within this perspective we can use our experiences, whether of failure or success, of victory or defeat, of embarrassment or pride, as openings to more of life's stages and as ways of receiving what they potentially have to offer. These passages, then, are passages to wisdom.

Quality aging is not simply life-prolonging but life-improving. To achieve this quality in aging we need the cooperation of all those who now conspire against it. This cooperation would include a change in attitude toward aging on the part of our culture. It would mean that the medical profession would continue its practice of not making age in itself a criterion for medical diagnosis. This cooperation would include also the churches in their increasing respect for the contribution to their communities of people in all of life's stages.

Finally, it would include a growing appreciation by older people themselves for repentance and forgiveness as a means not only of converting experience into wisdom but also of gaining a stature, a recognition, that is not based on the need to prove our worth. Through repentance and forgiveness we discover the value of being who we are.

CHAPTER 5
Positive Aspects of Aging

When I refer to the positive aspects of aging I am not avoiding the fact that aging ultimately leads to death. There can be a subtle, even subconscious, denial of human mortality at work in our resistance to the forces conspiring to program us for negative aging. Nor do I deny the possibility of becoming one of the frail old.

In a pertinent essay on aging, newspaper columnist Ellen Goodman contends that we do not prepare our children for the fact that someday we may need them. We do not have children anymore to take care of us in our old age. We assume in mid-life that we will always be able to take care of ourselves. We cannot imagine that we will ever be frail. Amazingly, we can feel this way even when our own aged parents in their frailness are needing us. "Our shame about aging prevents us from knowing and telling our children the dirty little secret of our human existence: When we too are old, we may need them—need to lean on them" ("Gravity of Age Pulls on Independence," *Chicago Tribune,* May 23, 1985, sec. 5, p. 4).

We have mentioned Malcolm Cowley's observation that those who write about the older years are in their late fifties or early sixties, "a time when most of them wanted to paint a bright prospect of their years to come; as yet they couldn't speak from experience" (*View from Eighty* p. 47). Ralph Waldo Emerson's essay "Old Age" was written when he was 57. It is optimistic and reassuring. One of his "benefits of aging" is that "age sets its house in order, and finishes its works, which to every artist is a supreme pleasure." But, says Cowley, what if the house burns down, as Emerson's did twelve years later, when his memory failed him? Shortly before he died, Emerson was taken to pay his last respects to his fellow New Englander and friend, Henry Wadsworth Longfellow, as he lay in his bier. Emerson's response on viewing the corpse was that, although he knew the man, he couldn't recall his name.

Emerson's optimism about life and the world made it difficult for him to see the shadow side of things. But it came to him even so. There is no escaping the tragic dimensions of the aging process.

Yet the shadows do not reveal the whole story. I recall a student interview with a woman in her early eighties who, when asked to reflect on her life and share what she believed to be her best period, said, "Right now!" There are positive aspects of aging, and these can be denied as well as the negative aspects.

Passages Into New Meaning

The positive aspects of aging are seldom acknowledged or even recognized in our culture. Evidently there are not supposed to be any. The aging process, as we have seen, is a series of *passages* that occur all through life. It was Gail Sheehy who publicized the term (*Passages*, E. P. Dutton & Co., 1976). For Sheehy, however, the passages end at mid-life. They occur approximately at ages 18, 28–30, 40, and 50. The years after 50 are not dealt with. When I read her book I was not only out in left field but out of the ballpark altogether.

As we have shown, our passages continue through mid-life into the senior years as well. The passage from the womb to the world begins the process, and the passage into death completes it. Each passage provides an entrance into a new context within which to experience life. For those of us open to receive, these passages not only enrich our experiences of life but add to our wisdom. For those closed in their minds, these passages only signal another period of increased rigidity and closed-mindedness.

Losses That Can Also Mean Gain

Aging is characterized by losses. As one grows older one's sensory perceptions may decrease. Hearing aids and bifocals are indications of this change. The sense of taste, as we have seen, is most likely to decrease considerably. One's agility, reaction time, and mobility may decrease. Older people frequently complain also of lacking the energy they once had.

These losses are frequently the butt of humor, and older people themselves may engage in it. At the 1985 Jack Nicklaus Golf Tournament Bob Hope, himself 82, told the story of an elderly golfer who could no longer see the ball after he teed off. So he took with him a fellow oldster with good eyesight. After taking a healthy swing at the ball, the poor-sighted golfer asked his friend, "Did you see where the ball went?" "Yes," the friend answered, "but I forget."

Ageist jokes, even when told by older people, stereotype the aged. They are like the Archie Bunker racist jokes. Yet humor can make the losses bearable. I witnessed my own father gradually lose his memory until he could no longer remember my name. The pain involved in witnessing this progressive mental deterioration was often assuaged by seeing the humorous side of some of his forgetting—such as when we thought he left his teeth on an airplane. But the humor does not *eliminate* the pain. Consequently it should not be used to *deny* it.

The losses of aging can also lead to gains. The loss of

a job, for example, or even one's forced retirement, can stimulate the search for something to replace it that may lead one into a new and sometimes even more satisfying career. "The best thing that ever happened to me," said an older colleague of mine, "was when I had to retire from this place. I was free then to pursue a dream I had had. I've had many rewarding experiences in this pursuit that I would never have otherwise had." This does not condone forced retirement on the basis of chronological age. It only demonstrates that God can use even what he may not will.

Psychiatrist Fritz Kunkel described this paradox of gain via loss by a diagram of two cones placed inversely within each other. The upright cone has an expansive base and gradually decreases in size until it comes to an end at its upper point. This cone represents our natural life, full of potential at birth and then, as aging sets in, gradually declining until it ends in death. The upside-down cone represents our spiritual life, beginning at its point with our birth and growing expansively, reaching its largest dimensions as our natural-life cone comes to an end. The second half of the spiritual-life cone encompasses the narrowing natural-life cone—thus indicating that in the maturing process the spiritual existence permeates and surpasses the physical existence. This illustration compares with the description in 2 Corinthians, which in like manner contrasts the natural and spiritual dimensions of life: "Though our outer nature is wasting away, our inner nature is being renewed every day" (4:16). "Every loss in the realm of the natural life," says Kunkel, "could and should be an adequate gain in the realm of the spirit" (Fritz Kunkel, *In Search of Maturity,* p. 287; Charles Scribner's Sons, 1951).

In one sense our losses due to aging are *packaging* losses. This is why aging is viewed almost entirely negatively by our culture. We put a great deal of emphasis on packaging—how things look. We like beauty, which includes bulging biceps, suntanned skin, cascading hair, cosmetic enhancement, and, above all, the fresh appearance of youth. But none of this is lasting. Søren Kierkegaard said, "Even that which, humanly speaking, is utterly beautiful and lovable—a womanly youthfulness, that is perfect peace and harmony and joy—is nonetheless despair" (*Sickness Unto Death*, p. 25). It is despair precisely because it is so transitory.

Motion picture actress Mary Pickford, "America's Sweetheart" of the 1920s and 30s, refused to be seen in public in her later years because she didn't want to disrupt her image. The older Pickford just didn't look like America's sweetheart any more.

Yet, at the same time that the packaging is changing, the essence within the package may stay the same or even improve. Losses lead to grieving. Some people deny their grief, others become fixed in it, and still others work through it. Healthy grieving prepares us to go on living after the loss. In this sense it is the process out of which may come the gain. Johann Sebastian Bach loved his wife and enjoyed her companionship. He left her in good health as he departed on a trip, but when he returned she had not only died but was already buried. It is hard for us in our day of communication technology to realize the shock Bach must have experienced. He grieved openly and lengthily. But he emerged from his grieving to go on living. "Life," he concluded, "is for the living." He later remarried, fathered other children, and wrote more beautiful music. "Blessed are those who mourn, for they shall be comforted" (Matt. 5:4).

Healthy grieving over our losses is a healing process. The quickest way to "get over the loss," if such is possible, is to go directly into the midst of the *pain* of loss and share this pain—expressing how you feel—with people who are understanding. While most losses can never be replaced, grieving over them leads us after a time to appreciate what we still have.

The most devastating losses are those of people we care about. While no one can replace our departed loved one and the relationship we have had, other persons and other relationships can help us to endure the loss. My mother had the remarkable ability to replace lost friends with new ones. When she died at 83 she had as many friends as she had ever had, the great majority of whom were younger—some much younger—than she.

The most devastating loss one may experience in aging is the loss of a spouse. To be bereft of a mate with whom one has shared life—parenthood, economic struggle, friendships—for fifty or sixty years is a loss that most of us would find utterly debilitating. The loss of a child, particularly in one's later years, can also be devastating. How can one continue to live—or why would one even want to live—without the significant relationship, in the few and very vulnerable years yet remaining?

Bereaved spouses have difficulty getting "permission" to grieve. Their children tire of hearing their laments and about their loneliness. The adult child's loss of the parent in question is a different kind of loss from that of the spouse. For most adults, parents are part of our past, so far as our present life is concerned. They do not usually play a vital part in our present or future plans. Intellectually at least we anticipate the loss of our parents. For the bereaved spouse, however, the loved one was a vital part of the present and future, as well as the past. Both present and future are now bleak. There probably is no replacement for this loss and the loneliness it creates. But community support—a network of family and friends who allow the bereaved to grieve— can help make the loss bearable.

The passages of the later years are also times of increasing limits. Yet limits are really nothing new. It is just that we experience more of them as we age. If you have had an experience like mine when I was 4 years old, you know what having new limits imposed on you meant way back then. For four years I was an only child, with my parents all to myself. Then came baby brother, and I had to move over. I'm sure I resisted this limitation of my former space, but I also believe I learned finally to accept it and to be happy that I had a brother. This was one of my earlier passages.

Accepting limits goes with being human. We are creatures of God and not ourselves the creator. While it has always been hard for us humans to be limited—we would prefer the unlimitness of being divine—we are the wiser for accepting our limited lot. It is part and parcel of dealing realistically with reality. In later passages these limits increase. At the same time they also have their positive side. In our young adulthood we may punish our digestive systems with junk food and alcohol, but this abuse becomes too costly in physical discomfort in later years. So we learn to discipline our intake of food and drink, and select our foods on the basis of more than taste. The gain is in self-discipline, which is worth far more to us as persons than our previous indiscriminate consumption.

As we age we have to give up old ego images—the macho man, for example, and the cute woman. We, of course, can exchange these ego-sustaining images for new images—the clever man, for example, or the shrewd woman. The greatest gain, however, would be to give up the need for *any* ego image—pictures of ourself that we need for our self-esteem—and learn instead to accept ourselves as we are, with no need for more attractive or more appealing image-projecting.

Freer from Cultural Demands

As we go through the passages of life, we can become increasingly free from the cultural demands on us to prove something—our worth, our competence, our success, our masculinity or femininity, our popularity. As these pressures lessen, we become more free to choose our *own* identity. As one enters the vintage years, the pressure is relatively *off*. The "score" for all practical purposes is "in." So it is less tomorrow that we are concerned about than today. The more we can live in the present tense, the more of life we receive. When our attention is riveted to a tomorrow in which big things will happen, we fail to focus on today and therefore fail to see what all is there for us in the present moment.

When the pressure to live up to one image or another lessens, we can relax our defenses. Since there is less to prove, there is a new freedom to *be* and to reveal who we really are rather than to project an image. Those who have experienced this freedom know what a relief it is to be free from the need to justify—to defend ourselves.

Greater Enjoyment

There is also the possibility of greater enjoyment as one ages. This would seem to be a contradiction in terms, since aging is often pictured as a time when enjoyment diminishes. What is there possibly to enjoy in the later years? The same enjoyments that were possible in the younger years! But younger people, under greater pressure to prove something, may find their enjoyment diminished by the tendency to identify joy with ego enhancement. When these pressures to prove are diminished, pleasure can become more purely pleasure. This is true even regarding sexual pleasure. The old myths of the decrease of sexual enjoyment in the later years have now largely been dispelled. Younger people simply assumed that sexual pleasure diminished with age, while older people who knew better were reluctant to talk about it. In today's more open society, the word has gotten out.

Yet many of us may not be ready to receive this information. We want to identify sex with the young.

The media depiction of sex for the young has had a brainwashing effect. It bothers us to think of older people with their aging bodies in sexual involvement. If older people buy into this shame trip for being sexual, they may cease being sexual. Dr. John F. O'Connor, a psychiatric specialist in the treatment of sexual problems, says, "In a culture that considers sexually interested older men as 'dirty old men' and sexually interested older women as ridiculous or pitiful—and all older people as generally worthless—high self-esteem is difficult to maintain," which in turn can only dampen one's sexual drive (quoted in Earl Ubell, "Upsetting an Old Taboo," *Parade*, Nov. 1, 1981, p. 5).

But as our acceptance of the passages of later life increases and older people listen to their own bodies and minds rather than to societal ignorance and rejection, the naturalness of sexual enjoyment may only increase with age. A couple celebrating their fiftieth wedding anniversary had the courage to say that the physical side of their life together was more important than ever. Mary Spock compared her sex life with 81-year-old Benjamin to that of a couple in their forties. Sex therapist Mary Calderone dispels the myth that one is born with a certain amount of sexual capacity, which can be used up by too active involvement in younger years. "The more you use it," she says, "the less you lose it—and that's not true of any bank account I've ever heard of" (ibid.). So it is probably true that those couples who have had a meaningful sex life in their early years will continue to have an even more meaningful one in their later years.

All other things being equal, which obviously is not always the case, sexual experiences in later years can become more enjoyable in and for themselves. Acts of intimacy are occasions of celebration rather than of achievement. The relationship is being celebrated; life as symbolized by sex is celebrated. The participants are receiving a gift, not proving their skills, and their response is gratitude rather than ego enhancement or deflation, depending on the outcome.

Could not these sources of pleasure have been realized in the earlier years? Of course! But cultural pressures regarding sex and other pleasures oppose this enjoyment. Far from allowing sex to serve its God-given purpose, our so-called liberated society has positioned sex into the same ego-dominating need to excel as it places other natural pleasures—sports, for example. The young are the most affected by these pressures to live up to expectations. Perhaps the most dominant of all pressures for the young is peer pressure, in the presence of which many find it next to impossible to maintain their own identity. But the passages of aging move us toward more freedom to be who we are, as cultural pressures are less threatening to our identity.

Even as sex is associated with our relationships, these relationships themselves can become more enjoyable for their own sake in the later passages. When there is less need for older people to prove anything, they themselves may have less need for others to prove anything either. The pleasure of the company of others is a pleasure in itself. John Sibley in his nineties experiences his highlight of the week on Saturdays. "I do an unusual thing," he says. "I have my family meeting every Saturday and have lunch together. You never know who's coming. But the value of family holding together pays off and is normal with us" (quoted in *Christian Science Monitor*, May 5, 1985, p. 7).

Deeper Insight Into Spiritual Realities

Along with increased enjoyment, the passages of aging may also bring a deeper insight into spiritual realities. The increased limitations of aging are potential stimuli for the development of *trust*. When our own powers lessen, our need for God becomes more conscious—even as the awareness of their own helplessness in their addiction can lead alcoholics to acknowledge their dependence on a Higher Power. Our painful limitations open our eyes to our identity as *creatures*—which we often tend to deny in our need to be unlimited—so that we recognize more clearly our indigenous dependence on the Creator. Trusting in the Power beyond our own is not an isolated activity. Rather, it shapes us into *trusting* instead of *controlling* persons, which in turn predisposes us to be trusting rather than controlling also in our human relationships.

Closely associated with trust is the capacity for *patience*. In our older years we learn to pace ourselves as we demand less from the present moment and experience more. Patience comes from the Latin *pati*, meaning to suffer, to endure, to be patient. Based on this root, Henri Nouwen identifies patience with focusing on the present moment, looking to it for meaning rather than to future moments, which would drain the present of all significance for us. The aging passages move us toward this patience since the future becomes much too shortened to contain our vision of meaning.

Trust and patience combine to produce *inner peace*. Among value choices, people in mid-life tend to give inner serenity top priority. By mid-life one's attention turns from subduing our outer world to bringing order to our inner world. Paul identified inner peace as the "peace of God, which passes all understanding," which "keeps"—literally, *protects*—our hearts and minds. This peace comes from letting our requests "be made known to God," in other words, from confidence in the Higher Power (Phil. 4:6–7). Since peace is one of those positive passions we seem to define largely by its opposite, war, it is difficult for us to define peace as a possession in and of itself. Peace is what stress authority Hans Selye calls a "good stress," coming from the security we experience in our relationships—with ourselves, others, and God. Peace "feels" good.

Since the increasing limits and losses of the later passages can lead us to depend more on the unlimited One, we find it natural to become more deeply involved in prayer as we age. In making our requests known to God, we are engaging in the *inner dialogue.* The loneliness that can mar the later years is mitigated by this relationship with God which, in contrast to all other relationships, is not terminal. Our investment in this relationship has sustaining value in this life as well as for our vision of the life beyond. Like Augustine in his *Confessions,* we do not indulge in introspection as a solitary exercise once we have learned to appreciate prayer. Instead we look within dialogically—in conversation with the Spirit.

As we age, our future shortens. Beside being a source of anxiety, this reality can also lead to a growing appreciation of the *eternal* dimension to life. This dimension, though connected with our present moment, continues to have meaning for us when this life in time has run its course. The eternal dimension to life provides the support we need in our aging for a positive vision of the future. This support need not be an escape from the reality of death and the pains of aging but, rather, can provide the context of meaning in which to face and bear these pains and realities. As one veteran of living put it, referring to his loved ones who had died, "I'm thinking more about eternal life these days. I suppose it is because I've got a lot invested there."

The perspective of eternal life that is not simply a mental escape from present unpleasantness is described as the Eternal Now. Rather than conceiving of eternal life as beginning when this life ends, the idea of the Eternal Now is associated with the present moment in time. Eternity breaks through the limits of time to change the character of time for those who are open to receive. The later passages in our life tend to move us into this openness. We get a glimpse into "the breadth and length and height and depth" of that love "which surpasses knowledge"—eternal in its fullness (Eph. 3:18–19).

I recall a friend's sharing with me that he was grateful to God just for *this* life. "If there is anything beyond," he said, "it will be icing on the cake." It is significant that he is not living in the poverty of the Third World but in the most affluent society on the planet. Still, even in the United States we can grow to appreciate eternal life as more than icing as we age. It becomes increasingly identified with our faith as we look to God for support in our losses and limits. The old, like the young, however, find their faith in eternal life continually beset by doubts. By the later passages these have become old doubts, with which we have learned to live. After all, we don't believe our doubts—otherwise they wouldn't be doubts.

Associated with this deeper insight into spiritual realities is the gift of values. As we live through life's passages, the trial-and-error method of learning begins to pay off. The spurious value system of workaholism, cutthroat competition, and materialism that characterizes our culture begins to reveal its shortcomings. Although it held the promise of satisfying our longings, this value system has failed to do so—in fact, we know now that it cannot do so. Our spiritual nature remains unsatisfied because spiritual values are not recognized. So we learn to discern the more important from the less important: the value of integrity over achievement, for example, and the value of persons over things, of life itself over what we accomplish in life, of our relationships over our possessions. A wise sense of values is truly a spiritual gift. Yet it comes to us through experience. Our priorities tend to change as we age. As the years accumulate, we become increasingly conscious of the fact that our destination for the second half of life is death. It is hard then to perpetuate a value system based on the illusion of our immortality.

This difference in values and priorities that can take place as we age is clearly seen in the way grandparents tend to differ from parents in regard to children. Of course, there are grandparents who take little interest in their grandchildren for one reason or another, and there are grandparents whose influence on grandchildren is actually harmful. But, by and large, grandparents seem to enjoy their grandchildren more than parents enjoy their children. This differentiation usually changes, however, when the grandparents have to function as parents. Having responsibility for the children seems to make a difference. Grandparents are not substitutes for parents. Ideally, in an extended-family model, they complement one another because of their stages in life.

Parents have a picture in their mind of what their child should be like, and they tend to evaluate the child by how close he or she comes to this picture. Grandparents have been through all this and do not need to fashion their grandchildren. There is less likelihood for the grandchildren to be extensions of their grandparents' egos. In a sermon he preached on the Old Testament practice of parents blessing their children, Henry T. Close reflected on his own childhood. "I know that for me, when I was very young and my parents were pressing me to be perfect, it was my grandfather who simply liked me. I still think of that as one of the most important influences of my life" ("A Blessing for Me," *Feed My Sheep,* Gregory J. Johnson, ed., p. 79; Paulist Press, 1984). Yet probably this same grandfather, as a parent, put similar pressure on his own children.

Young parents do not often appreciate the unconditional love that grandparents give their grandchildren. I must confess that as a parent I didn't appreciate it either. Yet I now view the difference as one of balance rather than conflict. In this perspective, grandparents are not only helpful but needed.

The positive aspects of aging are sufficient in themselves to create a more positive approach to our own aging. They are also sufficient in themselves to prevent older people from wanting to return—even in fantasy—to their younger days. Goethe wrote in his eighties, "I have some advantages which I would not exchange for the ones I had more of at forty. A plant would not want to return from the period of bloom to the time of leafing, or from the stage of seed and fruit to the time of blossoms."

Growing older is a meaningful journey, not a meaningless one. The last stages flow naturally from the previous ones. Death can be looked upon as the end of the journey. It also can be looked upon as a transition in the journey—another passage. Perhaps this is why *passing* is often used as a synonym for death. Yet the paradox remains. People do more than pass—they *die*. They end their life in this world—fully and finally. Yet death is also a transition, a passage, to the fullness of eternity.

CHAPTER 6
Spiritual Resources for Aging

When I was growing up, the model for aging for my family was an older relative named Marie. Marie lived with her married daughter and family, who seemed to enjoy having her with them. But as a child and later as a teenager I felt uncomfortable in her presence. When we visited she was always gracious, cheerful, and interested in me. What then made me uncomfortable? Her conversation. She never failed to ask me "Won't it be wonderful when we are with the Lord?" I obviously had to say yes to this question, but I wasn't where she was—spending most of her waking hours joyfully anticipating life in heaven.

Yet I can also say that Marie stands out in my mind even today as one of the most serene and joyful persons I have ever known. There is no doubt that her (to me) obsession with "the Lord" had much to do with her possession of these personal qualities. There was a light in her eyes. When in her nineties she began to fail and had to be placed in a nursing home, she continued to be radiant, joyful, and serene. While some older people remember the past best when their memory begins to fail, Marie's mind continued to be fixed on the eternal future.

Source of Security and Direction

I still feel more comfortable with people whose joy comes from their this-worldly experiences than with those whose joy emanates from their vision of the future. But while it was otherworldly in nature, Marie's joyful and peaceful spirit was a blessing to all who knew her. It had an amazingly *this-worldly* effect.

Marie was living testimony to the fact that believing in a caring Lord provides the inner security and sense of direction that is needed for growing older with meaning. She was thoroughly convinced that her relationship with God was not going to cease with her death. In fact, she anticipated just the opposite—that it would become even more wonderful and meaningful. She believed, with Paul, that "to live is Christ, and to die is gain" (Phil. 1:21).

Reflecting on his own faith in his senior years, theologian Joseph Sittler said, "The Christian faith is that if we live, we are the Lord's, if we die, we are the Lord's. This is a faith, not an empirically established truth" (Robert Herhold, "Probings by Joseph Sittler," *Christian Century*, Sept. 26, 1979, p. 917). This is a hard statement for our society. We tend to rely on truths proved by science and find it hard to speak of truth verified by faith. This applies especially to the possibility of life that survives death. We long for the assurance that there is such a life, but such assurance for us needs to come through the evidence of *sight*—of scientific verification (compare 2 Cor. 5:7). But nobody has returned after having died whom we can interview.

When I was a graduate student studying the phenomenon of extrasensory perception I spent several days at the Parapsychology Laboratory at Duke University under the directorship of Dr. J. B. Rhine. Rhine shared with me at that time that he had planned to study for the ministry but had lost his religious faith through his college studies in science and had become a biologist instead. But he never lost the desire for what he formerly believed. He entered the field of parapsychology, he said, largely in the hope of finding scientific evidence for personal survival after death. Only scientific evidence, in this case through the research of parapsychology, could bring him this assurance. Unfortunately, he said, he had not succeeded in establishing this evidence.

Although it has subsided to a large extent, there was a phenomenal interest shown in the stories of those who, though clinically dead, survived to tell of their experience. Collections of such stories in books like *Life After Life* by Raymond Moody, Jr., and Elisabeth Kübler-Ross's conversion brought about by such stories, stirred up much interest. The scientific answer was elusive. Were these people really dead? From a perspective of faith, however, this was not the critical question. Sittler puts it well: "Empiricism involved with this idea is quite irrelevant to what the Christian means by eternal life. If the church is going to say 'I believe,' then it must not try to say 'I believe, but I will believe better if someone will show me the real dope' " ("Probings," loc. cit.).

In wanting evidence other than that of faith, we are not really so different from other cultures and times. Job in his ancient setting also longed for this evidence as he faced what seemed to be his approaching death. "For there is hope for a tree, if it be cut down, that it will sprout again, and that its shoots will not cease. Though its root grow old in the earth, and its stump die in the ground, yet at the scent of water it will bud and put forth branches like a young plant. But man dies, and is laid low; man breathes his last, and where is he?" (Job 14:7–10). Then he asks the perennial question: "If a man die, shall he live again?" (v. 14). This is an individualistic question raised by one who lived in a group-oriented society, whose identity and even eternal destiny was associated with his tribe, his people. In our society we are highly individualistic and lack the collective context of Job's society. Yet

Job's sufferings lead him to feel just as alienated and lonely as we do in our twentieth-century Western civilization.

Like Job, we in our culture also seek to identify with nature. But where Job couldn't do it—humans are not like the tree that sprouts again from its dead stump—we seem to feel more comfortable with this identification. Because death is a part of nature, an indispensable part, and we are a part of nature, then death is natural to us and indispensable for our survival as a species. Ever since Ernest Becker received the Pulitzer Prize in 1973 for his book *The Denial of Death,* in which he demonstrated that we as a culture could not face the reality of human death, there has been increased interest in death and dying. A myriad of seminars and studies have been conducted in this area. The orientation of the great majority of these seminars and studies is this identification of humans with the realm of nature. Death is not only inevitable but necessary, and adjusting to it is a mark of both reason and maturity. Sharing our feelings about our own death openly with others is the way to reach this maturity of acceptance in harmonizing life and death. Acceptance of death in turn reduces our anxiety over it.

As healthy as this emphasis has been, and it certainly is an improvement over the denial process that Becker perceived, it represents only one side of the paradox in the human approach to death. We are a part of nature, and from this point of view, death is natural to us, and therefore needs to be accepted positively as a necessity for the continuance of the human community. But nature in terms of plants and animals is not the same as *human* nature. We humans protest death, even though we know that this protest doesn't make sense from a natural point of view. This protest is reflected in the popular response to Dylan Thomas's familiar words, "Do not go gentle into that good night. . . . Rage, rage against the dying of the light." Our experts on death and dying would say that this raging is a necessary stage in reaching a genuine acceptance of death. I am not sure that those who rage view their rage as therapeutic. It is rage for rage's sake! Death ought not to be, and I don't *want* to adjust to it! Death is the enemy! This is the Christian perspective. "The last enemy to be destroyed [by God] is death" (1 Cor. 15:26).

The preacher of Ecclesiastes described what may account for this paradox in human death. God, he said, "has put eternity into man's mind" (Eccl. 3:11). Unlike other creatures we humans recognize something about our mind, person, spirit, that is not destructible. To put the indestructible to death is the supreme injustice of the universe.

Behind our rage over death is our fear of it. Sittler sees this as basic to all fears. "The fear of death, I'm convinced, is at the bottom of all apprehensions. To say of any of us that we do not fear death is a lie. To be human is to fear death" ("Probings," p. 916). Interestingly, however, those who have had the experience of having "died" and then returned—such as described in *Life After Life*—insist they no longer fear death.

The anxiety over fate and death considered by Tillich to be dominant in the early centuries of the Christian era is not confined to that period. As we age, our era's dominant anxiety of meaninglessness and emptiness begins to coalesce with this anxiety over fate and death. Death becomes the symbol of meaninglessness. Fate is the arbitrariness of our destiny. As Tillich says, "Fate would not produce inescapable anxiety without death behind it" (*Courage to Be,* p. 45).

Remembering and Hoping

Perhaps it would be more accurate to say that God has put the *awareness* of eternity into our mind. The words that follow from Ecclesiastes indicate this interpretation.

"Yet so that [humanity] cannot find out what God has done from the beginning to the end" (Eccl. 3:11). The very thought of God, his eternal nature and works, is not really graspable by the human mind. Eternity is simply incomprehensible. Probably the closest analogy is the vastness of space, which, as an analogy, is also incomprehensible. Even the words "beginning to the end" are borrowed from time. What other language can we use? What other imagery? But it is not just that we cannot comprehend eternity, it is that we are *aware* that we cannot comprehend. This awareness is the result of God having put eternity into our mind.

Yet there have been breakthroughs to our understanding—what are called "fullnesses of time"—when the Eternal is manifested in time. So far as the people of the Old Covenant were concerned, the fullness of time was the exodus from Egyptian bondage. In the New Covenant it is the event of the incarnation, through which God initiated the exodus from the bondage of evil. "But when the time had fully come, God sent forth his Son, born of woman, born under the law" (Gal. 4:4).

In this event, which we celebrate at Christmas, God entered the human scene as the baby Jesus in order to overcome the power of evil and of death over the human spirit. The incarnation at Christmas leads to the resurrection at Easter. The resurrection was the good news for the first century A.D. because it spoke to the dominant anxiety of fate and death. Christ is risen! This news drew instant attention whenever it was proclaimed. It was in sync with the rising crest of the wave of the times. The revelation of a caring Power whom we know in the risen Lord replaced fate as the arbiter of our destiny.

There is a second fullness of time mentioned in the New Testament. "For he has made known to us in all wisdom and insight the mystery of his will, according to his purpose which he set forth in Christ as a plan for the fullness of time, to unite all things in him, things in heaven and things on earth" (Eph. 1:9–10). This is a future fullness—a culmination of time—when the eternal becomes all, and we humans are united together with God to fulfill his creative purpose. This is the hope that transcends death—the anticipation that gives meaning to all our pursuits in time. "As it is written, 'What no eye has seen, nor ear heard, nor the heart of man conceived, what God has prepared for those who love him,' God has revealed to us through the Spirit" (1 Cor. 2:9–10). The *past* of Christmas and Easter is tied to a *future* hope that provides us with the support we need as we age.

The past provides the basis for our hope in the future. So we remember the past—exercise this distinctly human gift of memory—to support our hope for the future. This is the purpose of festivals and feast days, when we recall our spiritual roots, remember those fullnesses of times when the eternal left its touch upon us. These times of remembrance reinforce our awareness of the eternal dimensions in our present moments, so that our hope for our future is strengthened. Remembering times are *meaning* times. Families gather together, congregations gather together, to celebrate their unity in the good news. The festival days help us to put our other days into the focus of our faith. They are beacons of light within the darkness of meaninglessness and death.

Ironically, these religious festivals are for some persons days of depression. Holiday blues are a common malady. What should be an occasion for family intimacy and hope only heightens loneliness and hopelessness when there is no family intimacy or hope to celebrate. Then the past only haunts the present, it does not enlighten it.

Because of the family orientation to these celebrations, they can be difficult times when a loved one is no longer present. Our family approached our first Christmas without our oldest daughter with much apprehension. Memories flooded in that only made her death more difficult to bear. My father's first Christmas without my mother was heavy for him, even though the rest of the family was present and trying very hard to provide the support he needed. Sensitive friends contact the recently bereaved during these festival days to let them know that they are aware of its pain for them.

These empty chairs at remembering times are reminders of death as the enemy. But the *events* that are remembered strengthen the hope that "death is swallowed up in victory" (1 Cor. 15:54). The festivals of the fullness of the time point to the fullness of time yet to come when God shall gather us all together—reunite us—as all things become united in him, "things in heaven and things on earth."

Belief in Providence

Believing in God puts the transcendent perspective into the way we see, think, and comprehend. Believing in God means believing in providence. Although providence means literally to *see* beforehand, it is usually used as a synonym for God's care. It is God's foresight that gives direction to his care. British psychoanalyst Ernest Jones said, "What one really wants to know about the Divine Purpose is its intention *toward oneself*" (quoted in Paul Pruyser, *The Minister as Diagnostician,* p. 64; Westminster Press, 1976). Believing in providence means believing that this purpose is *good.*

As we age, we are concerned about God's care for us in our growing dependency and ultimate death. Believing in providence means that God's care for us does not cease with our aging or even with our death. Not all of the religious leaders in Jesus' day were agreed on this. The Sadducees, who were the Temple priests, took the position that since the books of Moses did not mention the hope of eternal life, such hope was groundless. On this issue Jesus stood with the Pharisees, who affirmed the hope of the resurrection. Seeking to make this hope look ridiculous, the Sadducees brought a hypothetical case to Jesus of a woman who had had seven husbands in her lifetime. Whose wife would she be in the resurrection? After dispensing with the question by saying that marriages as we know them are not continued in eternity, he pointed to their own Scriptures for the testimony to the resurrection. "And as for the dead being raised, have you not read in the book of Moses, in the passage about the bush, how God said to him, 'I am the God of Abraham, and the God of Isaac, and the God of Jacob'? He is not God of the dead, but of the living; you are quite wrong" (Mark 12:26–27). Though Abraham and Isaac and Jacob, the patriarchs of Israel, were long dead when Moses heard these words at the scene of the burning bush, the patriarchs were referred to in the present tense: "I *am* the God of Abraham." The Sadducees had missed what to Jesus was an obvious assumption that the patriarchs were living even though they were dead.

The uniqueness of the Christian approach to aging is that the event of death, toward which the aging process is headed, is a transitional passage as well as an ending. The resurrection, Jesus affirmed, was to be his own experience following his violent death. The festival of Easter is the festival of not only remembering Jesus' resurrection, but of celebrating it as our own hope for resurrection. Jesus tied the two together himself when, comforting his disciples about his impending death, he said, "Yet a little while, and the world will see me no more, but you will see me; because I live, you will live also" (John 14:19). We are included! Paul expressed this same resurrection hope in the metaphor of a dwelling place. "For we know that if the earthly tent we live in is destroyed, we have a building from God, a house not made with hands, eternal in the heavens" (2 Cor. 5:1).

The goals fashioned by cultural values can leave us

unfulfilled even when we reach them. Though they are opposed to the values of the Christian faith, they nonetheless have a strong appeal. In spite of what Jesus said about our attitude toward possessions, our cultural values stem from the belief that our lives *do* consist in the abundance of our possessions. In contrast to Paul's observation that genuine power is made perfect in weakness, power in our culture's understanding is made perfect by controlling and dominating our own and others' destinies.

As we age we become more aware of how perverse these cultural values and goals are to the human community. They undermine our capacity for trust and elevate things over persons. In the generations of human history, we seem never to learn the lesson that these values take us in the opposite way for healthy aging and dying. It is difficult to believe in intangibles like love and trust and peace when the tangibles of possessions and power are so alluring. But the hopes these goals engender have a very short-lived period of satisfaction. What we need is a hope that takes seriously human mortality and frailty—a hope that cannot be destroyed by any decline or ending, especially the decline of aging and the ending of death.

Material things, of course, remain important to the elderly. Homes for older people that are sensitive to their clients' needs allow them to bring as many furnishings into their rooms as possible. For these things are not simply possessions. They are symbols of memories of people cared for and loved—of the human community of the past whose memory supports us in our present loneliness.

Belief in the providence of God is the way of receiving the peace that passes understanding—the inner serenity in which we are content to leave the control of our lives and those of our significant others in the "hands of God." But this peace does not come without a struggle. Even as joy is not without sorrow, so peace is not without disturbing doubts. In discussing the hope of eternal life with those who minister to aging persons, I was asked how this hope can be communicated without making it sound like "pie in the sky." I believe this can be done only by being honest with ourselves and others. Belief in eternal life is not only a leap of faith, it is *the* leap of faith of which all others are only reflections. No matter how well morticians do their work, there is a finality about a corpse—the finality of death. Only faith in the God whose care we have come to trust can carry our minds beyond this finality. And this faith needs continued support and constant renewal in order to affirm itself in the presence of nagging and sometimes overwhelming doubts. The peace of God is based on an *acceptance* of this struggle, as we look to God to sustain our faith when that leap of all leaps is before us.

This faith, however, is not without its evidence in our lives. To use the language of relational psychology, our *systems* are altered by this faith. For faith itself is a *system*— a relationship—the inner *dia*logue. While it exists in and of itself in our experience, our relationship with God affects all of our other systems as well. God is revealed through our relationships. Though he is beyond them, God is also "in and with and under them." To this extent these relationships are influenced and even shaped by our faith. This is a fact—a psychologically demonstrable reality, but one generally overlooked in systems psychologies and therapies. I refer again to Augustine's *Confessions* as a literal example of this faith system and how it affects our other relational systems. In reflecting on his mother, Monica, Augustine wrote:

> Receive, O God, my confessions and thanksgivings for innumerable things whereof I am silent. But I will not omit whatsoever my soul can bring forth concerning her, that handmaid of thine who brought me forth, both in her

flesh, thereby to be born to this temporal light, and in her heart, that I might be born again to the light eternal. They are not her gifts that I speak of, but thine in her. For neither did she give birth nor education unto herself, it is thou who didst create her; nor did her father or mother know what kind of creature was to be by their means.

Regarding his son Adeodatus, born out of wedlock, Augustine wrote:

> I confess unto thee thine own gifts, O Lord my God, who art the creator of all things, and abundantly able to reform all our defects: for myself. I had nothing in this child, but the sin wherewith he was begotten, for that we had care to bring him up in thy fear, it was thou and none other who didst inspire us thereunto. I do, therefore, but confess thy gifts. (*The Confessions of St. Augustine*, tr. by Sir Tobie Matthew, rev. by Roger Hudleston, pp. 232 and 229; London: Fontana Books, 1957)

Covenant of Calling

We are called by God as persons—individuals—and baptism is the mark of this calling. "Calling" is the Christian word for purpose, for meaning. We are called through our baptism to a purpose larger than what our own limited lifetime can encompass. Our baptism marks our dedication to this purpose. We are also a contributor to this covenant. If we are baptized as infants, our parents or other sponsors spoke for us, and if we were at the age of responsibility when baptized, we spoke for ourselves. Though our life is limited—"a mist that appears for a little time and then vanishes"—it is all we have (James 4:14). We need a purpose, a meaning, a calling worthy of a lifetime. Only a purpose that places our lives in the continuum of God's redemptive purposes for this world is sufficient to justify a lifetime of energy. The great tragedy we see about us is in the lives of people who are living for goals and purposes that sell them short, that leave them vulnerable to disillusion in the later passages when the bankruptcy of these goals becomes painfully evident.

Baptism also signifies that we are not alone in our calling. Baptism is a family rite or sacrament. We are baptized into a congregation, a local family of God. This family is our potential support system or network for living out our calling. The worship and witness of the congregation provides its fellowship with the transcendent dimension to their support one of the other, for we also are involved in supporting others in their calling.

Our calling does not cease as we grow older. We do not, we cannot, retire from it, even though we may retire from our job. Our calling is not identical with a job or even with our family roles. It can be expressed in other ways than through these familiar patterns. Our culture makes it hard for us to think of our calling apart from our work. The mission of the church provides us with opportunities when the familiar ways are not open to us.

A friend of mine who has been retired for a few years cautioned me not to retire to *nothing*. He and his wife have spent these years traveling about the country with a trailer attached to their car, visiting their children and planning their trips according to the seasons. But this has run its course, and they plan now to settle in one place. "What will you do then," I asked, "so that you don't retire to nothing?" He had already thought of this. "I want to get involved in a church," he said. "I have a couple of projects that I would like to try out."

So we continue to have a purpose, even in retirement, though it may be a less ambitious one. My retired friend has a Ph.D. degree in chemistry and held a responsible position in one of the "excellent companies" of our country. Yet it seemed to me that the idea of involvement in the church had as much appeal for him as did his job as a scientist. In fact, he is in a position now to take more risks for what he believes. He is free from the control of corporate interests and from the pressure of ambition.

Older people with their new freedom in their later years are in a position to take advocacy roles that younger people might find penalizing. In my own community, Ruth Youngdahl Nelson is a prime example. Chosen as Minnesota Mother of the Year in her earlier years, she became increasingly involved in the cause of world peace as her other responsibilities lessened. At the age of 80 and ill with terminal cancer she made the trip to the West Coast to join with protesters at the launching of the Trident submarine with the Polaris missiles. She fully expected to be arrested and jailed. Though others were arrested, she was not. Her age and illness made it possible for her to make her protest without the usual penalty.

Also in my community a middle-aged pastor led his congregation in some risky missions in their understanding of God's calling. Complaints reached the denominational headquarters, and a representative was sent to confer with the pastor. Instead, the representative was confronted by several older members of the congregation, who made it very clear that they not only backed their pastor but would continue to do what they believed was their calling as a congregation if the pastor were to leave. As a result, the pastor had to say very little; the older members took the responsibility for the ministry of the congregation.

Our baptism is also an antidote to discouragement in our response to our calling. If we receive too many discouragements, defeats, or disappointments as we attempt to carry out our understanding of our calling, it can *get* to us. When results do not come and we are buffeted by frustrations, there is the desire to give up. While visiting a mission field in Africa I listened to a veteran missionary nurse tell her story. It was a hard story with more frustrations than victories. "If I didn't believe I was called to this place, I would have quit long ago," she said. Her sense of calling kept her going. So when our sense of meaning needs buttressing and our efforts seem unrewarded, we need to say with Luther, "I am baptized," which in this instance means, "God has called me." It could be the help we need to hang in there.

Resource for Coping with Anxiety

Belief in God is a resource for coping with the anxiety of death and meaninglessness precisely because of the relationship or system that this belief sustains. The divine-human encounter is not only something in itself in our lives but it also permeates and influences all of our other relationships. In recent times we have been lumping all forms of anxiety under the category of distress or, simply, stress. As we go through the later passages of life, this stress is experienced largely as depression. Outwardly we appear flat, deflated, because we *are*. Inwardly, however, we experience the agitation characteristic of anxiety. We fear not only what *is*—the sense of deterioration under the burden of aging—but also what will happen to us in further dependency, dying, and death.

Stress in any of its forms accelerates the aging process. In young adulthood, in mid-life, and in the later years, stress has a negative effect on the functioning of our body organs and mental processes. In our later years, however, the cumulative effect of this stress abuse is more readily apparent. The sooner we are able to cope with stress, the better for the healthy functioning and retardation of the aging process of our bodies and minds. There is no more effective resource for coping with stress than believing in God, as the Higher Power with whom we can share our anxieties and in whom we can put our trust in our present and for our future. As we learn—and it is a learning process—to commit our lives to God as he is revealed to us in our human relationships, we experience in varying degrees the serenity of spirit that promotes the health of our bodies and minds. God's story in human history and in our personal history is the source for the hope that sustains us as we deal with the inevitability of our own death.

There is an eternal destination to our life story. We are going somewhere—"So there will be richly provided for you an entrance into the eternal kingdom of our Lord and Savior Jesus Christ" (2 Peter 1:11). This destination puts our journey in life into a larger perspective than simple identification with the world of nature would give us. It is this perspective that encourages us to grow older meaningfully.

CHAPTER 7
Examples
of Quality Aging

"Youth is a gift. Aging is a work of art." I read this somewhere but have forgotten where. It stuck with me because I like the idea of aging as artistry. Not all of us who age, however, are good artists. A woman in her eighties was found dead in her home. She had been dead *two years*. During this time nobody knew she was dead, even though her daughter and son lived in the same community. Since they were not on speaking terms with their mother, neither had made any attempt to contact her in those two years. Obviously there were no other contacts either—from friends, neighbors, or fellow church members. Hers was a tragic way to age—alienated, friendless, abandoned. Her life at its end was a far cry from a work of art.

Since all of us are not good artists when it comes to aging, we need role models in the art of growing older meaningfully. I have pointed to several people throughout the book—John A. Sibley, Claude Pepper, Ruth Youngdahl Nelson, my relative Marie, and others. Now I intend to focus on such models.

What kind of artistry is required for growing older meaningfully? Religiously speaking, the answer to these questions centers in the concept of calling. Examples of quality aging are those people whose sense of calling has kept their vision of faith vivid to the end. This faithfulness to the vision has shaped their lives into true works of art.

I have selected three such models upon which to focus. One of these I know from personal contact, another through correspondence, and the third I know only about: although I have seen him, I have had no other contact. They are Maggie Kuhn, Hulda Crooks, and Angelo Roncalli, otherwise known as Pope John XXIII.

The Advocate—Maggie Kuhn

Margaret E. ("Maggie") Kuhn spent most of her preretirement life as a professional lay church worker. When she reached the mandatory retirement age of sixty-five, she had to retire from her position with the United Presbyterian Church. It was this forced retirement that started Maggie Kuhn on the career for which she is now known.

She resented having to retire only because she had reached an arbitrarily chosen chronological age. So she founded the Gray Panthers to protest this and other societal injustices. The official description of the Gray Panthers is "Age and Youth in Action"—an integrated coalition to fight all kinds of discrimination. In 1984, for example, the Gray Panthers demonstrated on the steps of the Massachusetts State House to demand an end to the mandatory retirement age in that state, a demonstration at which Maggie was a key speaker. In this same year the Gray Panthers inaugurated a national campaign for peace, charging that war is ageist—this time in its discrimination against young men. In these and earlier protest demonstrations, Maggie has been forcibly removed by police on more than one occasion. The title of one of several books she has published *since* her retirement states clearly the purpose of the Gray Panthers and of Maggie Kuhn: *Get Out There and Do Something About Injustice* (Friendship Press, 1972).

Since her retirement Maggie has received seven awards: these include the Distinguished Service Award in Consumer Advocacy, the Peace-seeker Award, and the Justice and Human Development Award. She has developed a ten-step program for the Gray Panthers in preparation for an advocacy role, of which the first step is, "Our personal liberation from the Ageism of Society." As a preface to the ten steps, she describes the vision that launched the Gray Panthers: "Although society devalues us and wastes our experience by enforced retirement, we regard our experience as a positive good—the nation's largest untapped and unused human resource" ("Ten Steps to Prepare You for a New Advocacy Role," *Gray Panther Network,* Summer 1984, p. 5).

Since I had admired Maggie Kuhn for her advocacy leadership, I invited her to speak to our community. She spoke in a church with the largest seating capacity that I could obtain. Though those in the pews could scarcely see her head above the pulpit podium, her voice and presence soon filled the church. She shared with us her misgivings about senior citizen groups whose purpose is to secure benefits for themselves. Seniors, she said, are in a unique position "to work as advocates for the larger public good, as public citizens and responsible consumers." She also shared with us her own secret to quality aging. "I try to do at least one outrageous thing each day," she said—truly the stuff of which advocates are made.

The Balanced Life—Hulda Crooks

I first heard of Hulda Crooks when a reporter wrote a feature about her in our local newspaper. She had spoken at a county public health fair in a neighboring state. In his writeup, the reporter stated that Hulda had climbed Mt. Whitney for the first time at age 66 and for the twentieth time at age 85. What impressed me was not just the mountain peaks she had climbed but the peak experiences in her own life.

Abraham Maslow, in his study of healthy persons, discovered that one of the characteristics of healthy persons is that they have had peak experiences—that is, mountaintop or spiritual experiences. Often they are hesitant to tell others about these experiences for fear of being considered queer or mystical or even mentally unbalanced. Hulda Crooks epitomizes for me a healthy person.

I wanted to invite her to speak to my class in the Ministry with the Aged, but she lives in California. Instead, I wrote to her requesting that she write to my class, sharing with them her philosophy of quality aging. She graciously replied with a four-page single-spaced paper. The students responded warmly to her paper and sent her a personal thank-you note. We felt that though she lived far away she was still one of us.

Her paper contained insights such as the following: "A person looking to the sunset needs to feel its warmth and be cheered by the light of the sunrise beyond, when the trumpet shall sound to call him or her to arise and go home with his or her savior, never to be parted from his presence again." The spiritual side of our lives, however, also affects the physical. "The body thrives on being treated right. Over-nutrition and under-exercising are major problems of Western society."

The main part of her paper, however, was her Ten Commandments for a Rewarding Old Age. These reflect her holistic approach to life with its balance of the spiritual, mental, and physical. With her permission, I am sharing these with you.

1. Cultivate a spirit of gratitude and cheerfulness. It reacts on yourself and cheers others.

2. Eat sensibly. Use vegetables and fruits freely.

3. Exercise according to your ability.

4. Rest adequately.

5. Keep mind and body active. (To illustrate this commandment she described her experience in her walks to the university library of being accompanied by a man of 101 years who was "reading up on church history.")

6. Plan twenty years ahead.

7. Set your house in order. Take care of financial matters in case of emergency. That will ease the burden for those who must take over for you.

8. Get rid of material things you will never use. Keep your home or apartment neat, clean, and comfortable. Then you can enjoy having friends drop in.

9. Find something to do or someone to help. Being needed makes life rewarding.

10. Take care of your body the best way you can. Keep learning. Old age can be rich and full right up to the century mark.

Her conclusion: "We need to add life to years, not just years to life."

Hulda Crooks is a remarkable model of quality aging, considering what might have happened to destroy her artistry. She is widowed, living alone after many years of marital intimacy. Her only child died tragically of a drug overdose. Her balanced life sustained her in these traumas and continues to sustain her, probably because the center of this balance is a spiritual focus. The concluding words of her paper express this focus: "A firm faith in God is the answer to happy aging."

At age 89, Hulda is planning another climb up Mt. Whitney. In a recent letter to me in which she gave permission to use her material, she said, "In preparation for the Whitney climb I have increased my daily walking to an average of four to six miles. I have walked thirty to thirty-five miles per week for the last four weeks and feel more fit than before. Am keeping track of my mileage just for fun to see how much it will add up to in a year— by the time I am ninety!"

The Dreamer—Angelo Roncalli

Angelo Roncalli was the son of Italian peasants, and yet he learned to speak seven languages. Before he was ordained to the priesthood he was a sergeant in the Italian army. He tried to hide his gentle nature behind a thick mustache. Though his men sensed his compassion, they only gave him one occasion to impose discipline. Regretfully he imprisoned an insubordinate soldier. The following day all the soldiers had leave to go into town. When the sergeant saw the imprisoned soldier he asked him why he was not in town with the others. "But, sergeant," the man replied, "you gave me three days." "True," said Roncalli, "but I only meant evenings. In the daytime you can go out" (Kurt Klinger, *A Pope Laughs, Stories of John XXIII,* p. 113; Holt, Rinehart & Winston, 1964).

At age 77, as a cardinal of the Roman Catholic Church, Angelo Roncalli was chosen to be pope. As John XXIII he was pontiff for only five years; yet the quality of his papacy had little to do with his short tenure. As the *New Catholic Encyclopedia* acknowledges, he was considered to be merely a transitional pontiff—yet he introduced a new age. Henri Nouwen admits to having had a dim view of John. "I had seen the old, fat Cardinal Roncalli on a pilgrimage to Padua," he wrote, "and thought of him as an example of clerical decadence" (*Reaching Out,* p. 35; Doubleday & Co., 1975).

But in spite of what others expected, Angelo Roncalli had a dream, and that dream was the Second Vatican Council. He himself attributed his dream to the "sudden inspiration of the Holy Ghost." His goals for Vatican II were, first, to renew the religious life of Catholics and, second, to update the teaching, discipline, and organization of the church, with the unity of Christians as the ultimate goal. Although John delegated much of the work of the Council to others, he exerted his leadership at strategic moments.

John's pontificate is considered a turning point in the history of the Catholic Church. But John also changed the Protestant churches. Many of us can remember Protestant-Catholic relationships before Vatican II. Whereas each once viewed the other as something considerably less than a Christian brother or sister, after the Council each began to view the other *as* a Christian brother or sister.

I lived through the history that John made. I was in Dubuque, Iowa. Dubuque is two-thirds Catholic in population. The Protestants had a minority complex, the Catholics a sense of sufficiency, and areas of ignorance generated suspicion and separateness. All this was broken down by Vatican II. In an article for *The Christian Century*, I quoted the city manager, an Episcopalian who described the change: "In contrast to the past, we at city hall can pass with perfect ease from religious group to religious group. . . . In a community divided by parochial and public schools we have to work hand in glove, and this is what the religious breakthrough has accomplished" ("Dubuque's Experiment in Ecumenism," *The Christian Century*, Sept. 29, 1965, p. 1188).

Instead of the usual Protestant Reformation Service often characterized by anti-Catholic rhetoric, an Ecumenical Assembly was held at the Dubuque Senior High School, sponsored by the council of churches and the archdiocese. In a community with many interfaith marriages, tears were shed as these couples worshiped together publicly for the first time.

Perhaps of greatest importance, the breakthrough was manifested at a moment of crisis. Along with other

Mississippi River towns, Dubuque experienced the worst flood of its history in 1964. Spokespersons for the U.S. Army Corps of Engineers said that Dubuque was the best prepared city on the river. All that the city set out to save was saved. My family and I and other Catholic and Protestant families, together with Lutheran, Presbyterian, and Catholic college and theological students, filled the sandbags. The then mayor, a Catholic, summed it up well: "It would have been very difficult to achieve this sense of unity before. Since we were already in communication, we were able to go right to work with greater community spirit" (*Christian Century,* p. 1190).

The *New Catholic Encyclopedia* characterized the man responsible for all of this as follows: "He was gifted with an agreeable disposition and a ready wit, he was characteristically open and affable, understanding and compassionate, jovial and calm, familiar in audiences, hospitable, and a lively conversationalist" (Vol. 7, p. 1020). This was our family's observation also as we listened to John speak to the crowd in St. Peter's Square in Rome in the spring of 1959. Though we could not understand his Italian, we sensed his message. The people helped us by responding repeatedly with hearty and spontaneous laughter. He made everybody feel good, including us. This same jovial man revealed his deep spirituality in his *Journal of a Soul* (published posthumously by McGraw-Hill, 1964). An example is his prayer for Vatican II: "O Gentle Guest of our Souls, confirm our minds in truth and dispose our hearts to obedience, that the deliberations of the Council may find in us consent and prompt obedience" (p. 391). He had a dream at 77—and the world has been the beneficiary.

A Different Drummer

These models for quality aging are people who do not believe in our cultural approach to the aging process.

While the three on whom we have focused are or were ambulatory in their senior years, being able-bodied is not in itself a measure of quality aging. Neither is being able-minded. The spirit of the person is the crucial measure. My father, for example, was senile the last several years of his life, but because of his amiable and adaptable spirit he was able to live first by himself and later with my brother and his family—with visits to me—with a minimum of "burdening." Even as his mind faded, he never thought of himself as *old*, though he lived to be 90.

Those who are models for quality aging, who design an artistry of old age, listen to a different drummer. In the case of our three individuals, this different drummer is the call of God. They have demonstrated in their artistry the fallacy of our cultural interpretation of aging. At a social gathering, a middle-aged woman told me that after twenty years of smoking she had quit. Although she enjoyed smoking, she quickly recognized the wisdom of her decision in her increased physical vitality. "Since the average life span for women is seventy-eight," she said, "I am going to start smoking again at seventy-five. By then life is no good anyhow, and I might as well smoke again for pleasure." While she may have been speaking with tongue in cheek, she had also been brainwashed by the negative approach to aging in our culture.

It takes a strong ego—meaning a strong sense of identity—to follow another drummer. As Hulda Crooks said, "We are survivors." Our models are survivors of cultural discouragement. Their encouragement obviously had to come from another source. They—like the rest of us—had to choose sooner or later between the cultural seduction—which is also a put-down—to take it easy or to resist this pressure and choose instead to continue living a balanced life.

The courage to make the latter choice comes from knowing who we are—that we are called of God. As Paul put it, we have a dual citizenship. "But our common-wealth [citizenship] is in heaven, and from it we await a Savior, the Lord Jesus Christ" (Phil. 3:20). As sons and daughters of God we receive our identity from heaven and live out this identity on earth. Not only am I a child of God, I am a distinct individual, a unique member of God's family. The more my life is centered in the God who created and redeemed me, the more I become who I uniquely am. Rather than slowing down this process of individuation, aging can actually accelerate it.

What We Can Learn

What can we learn from our models for quality aging—those whose dual citizenship provides them with a security and freedom not possible by belonging only to this world? Although we could list many things, I will confine myself to two.

First, our models seek the improvement of life on earth. While their citizenship is also in heaven, their dedication is to the earth—and in particular to the human condition on this earth. They know from the Scripture that "it is more blessed to give than to receive" (Acts 20:35), and they will not permit society to cheat them out of this blessing. In the words of Maggie Kuhn, "We do not wear senior-power buttons or think of ourselves as special pleaders for the cause of old people."

But they are givers only because they are also receivers. And because they are receivers, they are grateful people. They realize that they *love* only because God *first* loved them (1 John 4:19). Since they have "freely . . . received," they are motivated also "freely [to] give" (Matt. 10:8, KJV).

Second, our models travel light. When I travel, the people who meet me at the airport are usually surprised by the small amount of baggage I carry. I do not need to go to the baggage claim area because I carry it all with me. I have had too many unpleasant experiences with checked baggage to risk it. But I also prefer to travel as little burdened by luggage as possible.

Our models have adapted this practice of traveling light to their whole life journey. Because they are not heavily invested in this world, they need take no more baggage with them than they can carry. While only one has taken the vow of poverty, each has stored up very little of the "treasures of this earth." They follow Hulda Crooks's eighth commandment, and rid themselves of material things they will never use.

Our models, therefore, exhibit a freedom in their artistry that is literally amazing. In contrast to what we see all about us and experience in our own lives, these people are relatively free from societal pressures to fashion who they are. They have resisted the trend to permit money, for example, to shape their lives. "Why did you retire early?" I asked a friend who had ceased to be enamored with the unmitigated leisure of retirement. "The company had such a good offer for those who had worked for them for thirty years that I couldn't refuse it." Of course she could have refused it! But she didn't. Why? Because, like so many of us, she assumed that the direction in which to move is indicated by financial advantages. Money, pensions, social security, or other "good deals" do not shape the artistry of the models of quality aging. They listen to a different drummer—one who maintained that a person's life is not measured by the abundance of his or her possessions (Luke 4:4). This drummer can be heard by each of us, since our citizenship is also in heaven.

CHAPTER 8
Investment in the Future

Quality aging can begin wherever you are in life. When my younger son was a graduate student in his early twenties, he found himself, like so many others in his situation, in a time bind. He wrote home, lamenting that between his studies and his other projects, he was getting only five to six hours' sleep a night, was skipping breakfast and grabbing whatever he could for his other meals, and had no time for physical exercise. I was troubled by this description of his life-style and wondered what I could do about it. Was there any use in saying anything? He had heard it from me before. I decided to give it a try, regardless.

I wrote back expressing my concern. "Why give yourself a handicap for your future?" I asked. On the basis that his present life-style had future implications, I emphasized the need for a nutritious breakfast, for adequate rest, and for disciplined exercise. To my amazement he *heard* me. He replied, saying that he had dropped a few items from his schedule so that he could give more attention to my suggestions.

Present Has Long-range Repercussions

I'd like to believe that he responded as he did not only because he believed that what I had said was true but also because he cared enough for himself to invest wisely in his future. How we treat our bodies—what we put into them and how we use them—has long-range repercussions. It is in truth an investment in our future. The writer of Ecclesiasticus in the Apocrypha saw this connection in its negative potential: "You have gathered nothing in your youth," he said, "how then can you find anything in your old age?" (Ecclus. 25:3).

There are cultural obstacles in the way of our investing wisely in our future. One is our society's approach to food. In a nation that could conceivably feed most of the world, we in the United States have malnutrition not only among our own poverty-stricken but also among our affluent. Eccentric billionaire Howard Hughes and Woolworth heiress Barbara Hutton both died at least partially of malnutrition—obviously not because of the scarcity of food but because of their own poor choices. Hughes and Hutton represent the extremes of a widespread perversity in our eating habits. The food processing of our giant food industry, together with our fast-food mania, has resulted in inadequate diets that accelerate the aging process.

As a prime example, consider what we have done to the grain from which we make our bread. As somebody has put it, "The biggest nutritional error of the century was taking the fiber out of wheat to make white bread." Now we are realizing how important this fiber is to our health, together with the wheat germ and other ingredients we had eliminated. Yet in spite of this knowledge many people still use only white flour products.

Churches should be leading the way in restoring our diets to food as God has prepared it. Yet they are instead a leading source of temptation. How many churches, in their coffee time on Sunday morning, continue to serve only doughnuts and sweet rolls? I visit many churches, and I have yet to see fresh fruit or whole wheat crackers as an option. A church camp for youth that I recently attended served only white bread and no fresh fruits or vegetables for the entire session. Instead what we were served was largely processed food—instant mashed potatoes, Tater Tots, frozen pizzas, and the like.

We can be grateful that our government requires that manufacturers of processed foods and drinks list the ingredients of their products on the packages in the order of their amount. It is wise to read this list of ingredients before you make your purchase. Buy bread, for example, that lists *whole* wheat flour first (and not just wheat flour), margarine that lists *liquid* rather than hydrogenated oil first, and, in general, foods that list little or no sugar or salt or chemical additives. Good foods are in our stores. It is we who need to be selective.

Another obstacle in the way of quality aging is our society's love affair with the automobile. Although we are improving in this respect, many of us wouldn't think of walking five or six blocks if we could drive. The result has frustrated our body's need for exercise. The day of reckoning comes as we grow older. Osteoporosis, for example, a bone disease that causes older people's bones, particularly women's, to become brittle and their stature to shrink—is now recognized to be due in part to lack of exercise as well as calcium deficiency.

Most of us know of an older person who has fallen and broken a hip or leg, and whose whole life has been negatively affected as a result. Falls are the fourth most common cause of death in the United States and approximately 75 percent of them occur in people over sixty-five. But Dr. Gisele Wolf-Klein, geriatrician of the Falls Clinic at the Jewish Institute for Geriatric Care in New Hyde Park, New York, maintains that "falls are not a normal part of aging and may be manifestations of the onset of disease." Older people have slower reaction times, which may contribute to the possibility of falling and also to their fear of it. Yet even this reaction time can be helped. As the Falls Clinic points out, "Exercise can help increase alertness, coordination, good posture, and muscle strength" ("Falls, Big Fear of Elderly," *St. Paul Pioneer Press,* April 17, 1983, p. 9D).

Dr. James Reinersten, president of the Park Nicollet Medical Foundation in Minneapolis, Minnesota, agrees. "Only 30 percent of those over sixty-five exercise regularly," he says, "and this lack of activity may accelerate some of the most debilitating changes associated with aging." Dr. Reinersten also noted that "hip fractures from falls are more likely among the elderly who are obese, weak, and lacking in coordination—factors associated with a sedentary life-style." Even mental alertness declines among the physically inactive. His conclusion is that fewer older people would suffer disability or need institutional care if they remained physically fit. In fact, admissions of the elderly to such institutions could be reduced 20 percent, he maintains, by a widespread participation in fitness programs ("Try to Stay Fit to Avoid Disability," St. Paul *Dispatch,* June 15, 1985, p. 8A).

In spite of this evidence we continue to discourage older people from walking and instead offer them rides in our automobile. It would be much better for them and for those who offer the rides if they would walk together to their destination. If you are an older person and able to walk, the next time some well-meaning person offers you a ride, suggest instead that you walk together. You will be doing your friends a favor in their own investment in quality aging. We are usually more likely to keep fit in later years if we have begun to do so earlier. My older son ice-skates with an 84-year-old man who has been skating almost daily for twenty-five years. He has won every prize available in figure skating for his age group and now is looking forward to another prize—in the 85 to 90 bracket.

This same need for exercise is true also for the brain. Although the brain's weight is as much as three ounces less by age 60, older people can learn as well, even if more slowly, as they did in their youth. Even the loss of millions of brain cells cannot impair a brain that has a trillion such cells. Those who have studied the brain insist that the main need for continued brain functioning is to keep the brain stimulated. "Using it means not losing it" (Gina Maranto, "Aging, Can We Slow the Inevitable?" *Discover*, Dec. 1984, p. 21). Dr. Lissy Jarvik, a psychiatrist with the University of California, in a study of men and women tested periodically as they grew older, found that those who kept active mentally did best in retaining their cognitive ability. "The activity need not be scholarly," she said, "it could be reading the newspaper, listening to the news, reading books or magazines, playing cards or playing shuffleboard" (ibid.). Her conclusion: intellectual activity in most cases remains relatively intact in old age when one keeps the mind involved and functioning. (Mental exercise, however, will not protect against brain diseases like Alzheimer's.)

Lazy brains, like lazy bodies, contribute to mental and physical deterioration. By the same token, active brains and active bodies contribute to mental and physical fitness. I was the youngest pastor in my pastoral conference when I began my ministry, and the oldest active pastor was in his early eighties. Dr. Robert Golliday had distinguished himself by his published sermons and ecclesiastical leadership during his long ministry. Since I was a new colleague in the ministerium, he reached out to me with support and encouragement at every opportunity. But the example that stuck with me was his habit of taking a course in philosophy each year at the university, *for credit*. He was doing this in his eighty-second year while serving as senior pastor of his congregation. No wonder his sermons continued to stimulate his congregation!

Recent studies have indicated that if one begins after age 65 to eat properly and to exercise regularly, one probably will not add any more *years* to one's life. For this to happen we need to begin earlier—the earlier the better. Yet these same studies indicate that even after 65, changes in life-style will improve the *quality* of life. Perhaps it is similar to bypass heart surgery. Current evidence indicates that there is no appreciable addition to one's life span through this surgery, but many of those who have had it not only feel better but are better able to function after having their arteries unplugged.

Our decisions are frequently made on the basis of what will improve our life, not necessarily what will lengthen it. Dr. Richard Greulich, the National Institute on Aging's scientific director, says that the goal of the NIA is "to improve life rather than to extend it," since their interest is in "the quality, not the quantity of life" (*Discover,* Dec. 1984, p. 21). What does it profit us to live to advanced years if we are not really living in those years? Ironically, however, if one's life is satisfying and fulfilling, this in itself is an antiaging influence and therefore a contributor to a longer life span.

The effect of life-style on the aging process is summed up by researchers Donald Morse and Lawrence Furst as they list the physiological changes in aging and then qualify these changes by life-style habits.

> A decrease in the number of normal functioning cells: some of these changes may be due to overwork and abuse.
>
> An increased amount of fat: probably preventable and relates to too high a caloric intake vis-à-vis the amount of exercise done.
>
> A decrease in the amount of oxygen taken in by the lungs and used by the tissues: but apparently some [of these changes] are caused by the lack of exercise and poor nutrition of the aged.
>
> A reduction in muscular strength: a good part of this change could be due to the inactivity of aged people.
>
> Decreased functioning of endocrine glands (those that produce hormones): part of these changes may be related

to lack of exercise and mental withdrawal that occurs in many of the aged.

Decreased functioning of the immune system: but many physically and mentally active octogenarians show little evidence of immunological deficiency.

Aging affects the brain and central nervous system, but some of the deleterious effects are caused by atherosclerosis, alcoholism, lack of exercise and decreased use of mental faculties. (*Stress for Success*, pp. 140–142; Van Nostrand Reinhold Co., 1979)

Spiritual Focus

The investment in our spiritual development provides a basic motivating force for living that is conducive to healthy aging. A devotional perspective integrates us into the transcendent dimensions of human living. In the words of Paul, "You are not your own; you were bought with a price. So glorify God in your body" (1 Cor. 6:19–20). While Paul is referring to using our bodies in sexually moral ways rather than in immorality, the larger context of caring for our bodies is implied. They are the "temple of the Holy Spirit within you" and deserve respect. Since we belong not to ourselves but to God, who has redeemed us with the sacrifice of the cross, our bodies also belong to him. We glorify God when we treat and use our bodies respectfully—that is, healthily.

The spiritual focus in our life is the center that puts everything else into place. God's providential care gives us a consistent sense of meaning amid the vicissitudes of our lives. We are in God's hands, and our commitment is to God's call. The awareness of the Spirit's presence in the temple of our bodies provides us with the closeness, the communion, the inner dialogue, that counteracts the loneliness that might otherwise take over in the losses of later life. We are called by God to fulfill our potential as believers, physically, mentally, and spiritually. It is not only our business; it is God's business.

This spiritual focus in our living produces the feedback of positive passions. Living purposefully stimulates the feelings that feel good—peace, enthusiasm, joy. These are *good* stresses because they are good for us—spiritually, mentally, and physically. The more of them we experience, the better. These good stresses counteract the bad stresses—depression, anxiety, resentment. These are bad because they are bad for *us*. As Hulda Crooks says in her letter, "They affect our circulation, upset our digestion, disturb our sleep, raise our blood pressure and rob us of the joy of living." In contrast, the positive feedback from a spiritual focus, the "fruit of the Spirit," slows the aging process because it does the opposite for us from the bad stresses. "The fruit of the Spirit is love, joy, peace, patience, kindness, goodness, faithfulness, gentleness, self-control; against such there is no law" (Gal. 5:22–23). They need no rules and laws to restrain them because what they do for us—and others—is good.

There is nothing new in this discovery that the positive passions are good for our total health. The biblical proverb "A cheerful heart is a good medicine" shows that this awareness has been around for a long time. So also the effects of the bad stresses: "A downcast spirit dries up the bones" (Prov. 17:22). Dr. C. Ward Crampton—whom some of us may still recall with affection as the helpful writer on physical fitness in *Boys' Life,* the Boy Scout magazine, and who later became a noted geriatric specialist—devised a five-point program for the life enrichment of older people for the YMCA. The fifth point was "Praise God!" Praising God is an expression of good feelings. It combines gratitude, worship, and positive involvement.

Yet—not always. "Praise the Lord" has become for some a ritual for repressing what they do not want to face. By compulsively expressing their praise of God, they hope thereby to lose awareness of the doubts, fears and resentments, and guilt that may be eating away at their spirit. This ritual can also be used as an evasion from facing or dealing with the evil in our society. This kind of "praising God" can make us sick rather than well.

But when praising God comes from the realization of God's goodness in spite of our own and others' evil, then it is a worshipful expression of gratitude. Praising God in this understanding is not only good for the aged but also for the middle-aged and the young as well. Indeed, it is good medicine; it is also a symptom of good health. There is wisdom in the old collect: "Grant us, O, Lord, with all thy gifts, a heart to love and praise thee."

This spiritual focus to our lives helps us to learn from our experiences. "The fear of the Lord is the beginning of wisdom, and the knowledge of the Holy One is insight" (Prov. 9:10). Wisdom comes from experience within the perspective of faith. It is this wisdom, as we have noted, that older people whose lives are spiritually focused have accumulated through their years of experience. "What an attractive thing is judgment in gray-haired men, and for the aged to possess good counsel! How attractive is wisdom in the aged, and understanding and counsel in honorable men! Rich experience is the crown of the aged, and their boast is the fear of the Lord" (Ecclus. 25:4–6). This appreciation from Ecclesiasticus of the wisdom of the aged, except for the exclusive language, needs once again to be heard. This is the wisdom of experience that Maggie Kuhn called the "largest untapped and unused human resource." Ecclesiasticus even then warned against devaluing it. "Do not disregard the discourse of the aged, for they themselves learned from their fathers; because from them you will gain understanding and learn how to give an answer in time of need" (8:9).

The spiritual focus of the individual is inescapable from a Christian viewpoint from the fellowship of believers which Paul called the "body of Christ." The very nature of *body* implies an interdependency in which older people can continue to be givers even as they receive. This fellowship with those who share our faith is indispensable for healthy aging because it supports our spiritual focus in the losses and limitations that can afflict us in the later life stages. Here is our experience of belonging in the midst of loss. Here is our support in the midst of limitations. We need *people* as we age—people who care about us and for whom we care. The church— as the local congregation—offers the best available op- portunity for this needed social support in our otherwise solitary journey through life to death.

Working on Our Artistry

Working on our artistry of aging is a whole life process which we carry out under God. The goal is sufficient in itself to motivate us to give it our all. The prize for living in harmony with the laws established by the Creator— "Laws which govern every enzyme, cell, gland and organ"—is health (Hulda Crooks's letter).

But there are no guarantees. "Living in harmony with the laws established by the Creator"—following the life-style for quality aging—is simply doing what we can do to influence what happens to us in our life. These activities will *always* help, but they may not always be sufficient to prevent what we are trying to avoid. Some factors that contribute to good health in the later years are not under our control.

Our heredity is one such influence on our lives. We obviously had no choice in the genes that we received from our parents. Our exposure to disease is another. We may only discover the exposure after we have experienced it. Whether our immune system is up to the exposure may depend on factors other than our health habits. Our vulnerability to accidents is yet another factor. Accidents may be due to the carelessness of others as well as of ourselves. Health hazards at the workplace may not be recognized in time to prevent damage. The greed of others may even obstruct the research needed to determine the risks. I have a friend who exposed himself to cancer every time he used a particular chemical at his job. He didn't realize the danger. Yet this ignorance did not prevent his contracting the disease.

These are facts we can recognize because they have happened. But what is it that we do not yet know? What dangers are we in now that are yet unrecognized? What stupidities are being perpetuated by the professionals to whom we must commit ourselves when we are afflicted in one way or another? A former student of mine was treated for a disease several years ago in what is now recognized as a primitive and dangerous way. Yet it was the best way that was known then. But this did not prevent the health problems that have disrupted his life as a consequence.

Researchers in aging are studying the various "clocks" that tick away the time that ends at death: the genetic clock and the hormone clock are two such measures, and there may be others. What happens to us when these clocks are ticking at different rates? In addition to these clocks is the process of bodily wear and tear, over which we have some, but not total, control. Can this process affect the ticking of the clocks? There is a good possibility that it can (*Discover*, Dec. 1984, p. 19).

In this process of aging we are obviously not dealing with a simple cause-and-effect relationship, such as "good nutrition leads to a healthy old age." Rather, we are dealing with an assortment of factors, some known and some yet unknown, some of which we can control and some over which we have no control, which must synchronize—come together in some sort of simultaneity—to produce the effect. This larger picture of cause and effect helps us to cope with the shock of an Adelle Davis, with all her knowledge of diet, dying of cancer at 70, and Jimmy Fixx, with all his disciplined running, dying, not just at 52, but dying while running! Their early deaths were surprising only to those who believe they can control their time of death by their life-style. If we can control the cause, we believe we can then control the effect. But the causes are multiple, and their synchronization is important. Any of the good things we are doing, including our devotional activities, may not be sufficient in themselves to guarantee an effect. But they are a help in this direction, and they may be *the* crucial factor or factors.

To conclude, the healthy life-style described in this chapter is something we can do—and something for which we are responsible. Although the life-style may not be sufficient in itself to ward off the disabilities sometimes associated with aging, it will *help*. It will also affect the quality of life in our vintage years, regardless of the limitations of aging. We are responsible to ourselves, of course, to live the style of life that invests well for the future. We are also obligated to do so for the persons with whom we live or with whom our lives are closely related and for whom we care. We are responsible also to God—to whom we belong—who has called us to this life-style as a way of using the gifts he has given us.

Conclusion

Growing older meaningfully is a lifelong investment—an example of self-care or self-love in its most wholesome sense. It is an example also of caring for others. Recently I greeted a neighbor who was swimming laps at our local pool. "What brings you here?" I asked. "I'm tired of paying for people who don't take care of themselves," she said, "so I decided to set a good example."

Few of us live only to ourselves. So the excuse one often hears regarding self-destructive behavior—"I'm only hurting myself"—is simply not possible. Writing in our newspaper, a young woman lamented the death of her mother, whose debilitating illness was related to her heavy smoking. "Mother always said she was hurting only herself when we pleaded with her to stop smoking," she said. "My grief and that of my brothers and sisters and father over these past months is painful evidence that she was *not* hurting only herself." The comparison of the Christian fellowship to the human body illustrates this relationship. The functioning or malfunctioning of each member—organ—affects the others. "If one member suffers, all suffer together; if one member is honored, all rejoice together" (1 Cor. 12:26).

Growing older meaningfully is an activity in caring because we live better for the effort—and we, our intimates, and our community receive the benefits. We may also possibly live longer as a result. But living longer is only meaningful if we are also living better. Yet, as we have seen, living better can contribute to living longer— as one factor among others—simply because living better is good for our bodily, mental, spiritual, and social functioning; it slows the wear and tear on body organs and contributes to the vitality of our relationships.

Growing older meaningfully is a way of *living* meaningfully. Actually, it is an *investment* in meaning. Meaning is implicit in the order of the universe—the laws of our physical nature, of our social interactions (ethics, morality), and of our spiritual development. Living by these laws simply makes sense, since we as well as those for whom we care are the beneficiaries. Growing older meaningfully is an example also of our care for God— whose laws we respect in response to his call to be good managers of all that he has given us.

Yet meaning goes beyond the meaning implicit in the order of the universe, for there is disorder also in the created world. Meaning in the laws of nature needs to be seen within the context of ultimate meaning—the meaning focused in God, which encompasses death and eternal life. Meaning, thus, centers in *faith,* which goes beyond the order and disorder of the universe.

Investment in meaning is based on a logic different from that which sustains our cultural values. In contrast to these values, the logic of our faith is not based on making ourselves secure by acquiring power or possessions. What does it profit if we gain the whole world of power and possessions and lose our own selves in so doing? For the self—your self, my self— as we have seen, develops in a direction opposite to the deterioration of the aging process. This self—yours and mine—needs to give itself to the larger context within which our life is lived—namely, to the Christ through whom the call of God has come. "For whoever would save his life will lose it; and whoever loses his life for my [Christ's] sake, he will save it" (Luke 9:24).